ETHNO-SOCIAL CONFLICT AND NATIONAL INTEGRATION

ETHNO-SOCIAL CONFLICT AND NATIONAL INTEGRATION

P. N. RASTOGI

GYAN

GYAN PUBLISHING HOUSE

NEW DELHI-110002

ISBN 81-212-0443-7
Library of Congress Card No. 93-900301

Published in 1993 by
Gyan Publishing House
5, Ansari Road, New Delhi

Composed by Ideal Computers Pvt. Ltd.,
and printed at Goyal Offset Works, Delhi.

CONTENTS

PREFACE

Ethnic schisms, tensions, and conflict, constitute a serious problem situation for the Indian society. This problem situation is not only large, complex, and difficult, but its severity has also been growing in the recent years. Ethnic antagonisms and violence threaten the very unity and survival of the nation. The problem has received a great deal of attention in the context of its dangerous implications for national integration. Its nature and dynamics, however, remain poorly understood. The efforts toward its solution have remained unproductive.

Present work attempts to understand and explain the problem of ethnic conflict as a generic problem phenomenon besetting most plural societies. The analysis further proceeds toward identifying the requirements of monitoring and problem solving, and derivation of verifiable predictive inferences. An integrated dynamic model of the problem consisting of highly interacting feedback cycles, is developed for this purpose. Situations of ethnic opprobrium in Indian, as well as, other plural societies are seen to be the empirical, isomorphic variations of the problem's basic dynamic structure. The isomorphism extends to their solution also.

Short term and long term policy measures for the resolution of the problem are identified from its dynamic multi-cyclical structure. Explanation, prediction, monitoring, and control, of the problem situation emerge as inter-related phases of an unified pattern of social cybernetic analysis. The analysis enables one to uncover the 'what', 'why', 'how', 'when' and 'what needs to be done' aspects of ethno-social conflict and its obverse of national integration. On account of its grim and dark nature, inter-group conflict is also viewed as part of the larger problem of human misery and suffering in social systems. The lasting solution of the problem is thence seen to be embedded in the solution of the larger problem of human misery.

Support for carrying out this study was provided by the Quality Improvement Programme of the Ministry of Education at the Indian Institute of Technology, Kanpur. Thanks are due to them for making this work possible.

P.N. RASTOGI

1

OBJECTIVES AND OVERVIEW

The problem of ethnic tensions and conflict in Indian society is large, complex, and difficult. It is in fact a crucial problem in almost all pluralistic societies. Ethnic antagonisms and violence threaten their very integration and survival as national society systems. The actors, events, situations, and interactions between opprobrious ethnic collectivities may differ both within and across societies in terms of their specific socio-cultural and politico-economic factors. A common underlying dynamic pattern of the phenomenon is nevertheless discernible across the variations of ethnic conflict in space and time.

Present work attempts to understand the nature and dimensions of ethnic conflict and the related problem of national integration. It endeavours to identify the underlying factors and the nature and pattern of their interactions that lead to the emergence, growth, and persistence of ethnic antagonisms in societies. It also endeavours to derive predictive inferences from the analysis. The analysis further proceeds toward identifying the requirements of monitoring and control for problem-solving. An integrative dynamic representation of the phenomenon is developed for this purpose. This representation is in the form of highly interacting positive and negative feedback cycles. The analysis is based on the methodology of social cybernetic analysis (Rastogi,1973, 1979, 1990, 1992). Situations of ethnic opprobrium in pluralist societies are analysable in terms of the problem's generic dynamic structure. They are seen to be the empirical isomorphic variations of the phenomenon's basic dynamic structure. The isomorphism extends to their solution also.

Solution to the problem of ethnic conflicts is the basic pre-requisite toward achieving the goal of national integration. The concept of national integration, however, goes further and deeper than the mere control of opprobrious ethnic relations. The latter represent a short term approach toward the more basic goal of national integration. The long term approach toward achieving the goal involves resolution of the core problems of self and identity of the members of culturally different and proud ethnic groups. Such a resolution in turn, can be possible only in terms of a commonly shared framework of transcendental values, norms, and purposes. The nature of such a framework, and the requirements for the problem's long term solution and the means thereof, are explicated towards the end. Explanation, predictive inference, and problem solving measures emerge as inter-related facets of an unified analysis in the present study. The study also seeks to bring out the 'missing link' of the ineluctable spiritual factor for sustaining the health of social systems.

In the light of the foregoing discussion, the objectives of the present inquiry in more specific terms may be listed as follows:

OBJECTIVES

[I] What is the nature of the situations of ethnic tension and conflict?

[II] How and why do such situations arise, persist, and grow? What are their consequences?

[III] Does the phenomenon have a generic structure across plural societies of the globe?

[IV] What is the nature and dimensions of ethnic schisms in Indian society? How may they be understood in the comparative context of other pluralist societies?

[V] What is national integration? What are the basic issues involved in achieving it? What is the significance of these issues?

[VI] Why have the country's efforts toward the promotion of national intergration failed? What are the deficiencies and flaws of national policies in this context? What are the requirements for fostering integration?

[VII] How may the situations of ethnic opprobrium involving violence be monitored and controlled?

[VIII] What are the short and long term solution perspectives toward coping with ethnic conflicts?

[IX] How may the problems of ethnic schisms and national integration be resolved in a steady state manner?

These objectives show that this study attempts to combine the theoretical analysis of a complex socio-political phenomenon with the derivation of inferences for practical application toward problem solving.

These objectives are sought to be realized through a set of seven chapters including this one and two appendicies. An overview of the volume's chapter scheme may be provided as next.

OVERVIEW

Chapter two, i.e., the next one, outlines the major ethnic schisms of the present day Indian society. They are seen to be based on the divisive cleavages of caste, community, language and religion. Ethnic violence and terrorism dominate the social scene in Assam, Kashmir, and Punjab, while high levels of ethnic tensions prevail in other parts of the country. The scenario of ethnic conflicts in Indian society is also juxtaposed with analogous types of situations in other plural societies of the world. The situations of ethnic opprobrium in Sri Lanka, Burma, Pakistan, Phillipines, Cyprus, North Ireland, Yugoslavia, and African countries are briefly outlined in this context. This chapter serves to bring out the widely prevailing nature of this pathological phenomenon in various societies of the world.

Chapter three examines the nature and functions of terrorism as a major form and symptom of acute ethnic conflicts. The psycho-social bases of terrorist violence are briefly elucidated. Chapter four develops and presents the common underlying dynamic structure of the phenomenon independent of its occurrences in space and time. This structure is seen to consist of a number of highly inter acting positive and negative feedback cycles. It enables one to understand the how and why of the emergence, growth, and persistence of the situations of ethnic opprobirum. It thence also serves to provide a basis for identifying the nature and requirements of the problem's resolution in a generalized context.

Chapter five examines the nature and meaning of the concept on national integration. It defines concisely the issues involved in achieving national integration in pluralistic societies in general and the Indian society in particular. It also brings out the flaws and deficiencies of the state policies for the promotion of national integration in the Indian societal system.

The integration of a nation cannot be achieved in the absence of harmony and cooperation between various ethnic groups in its population. The solution of the problem here calls for both short term and long term measures. The short term measures are primarily concerned with controlling the situations of violent ethnic conflicts on the one hand, and preventing the aggravation of ethnic opprobrium on the other. The requirements for the monitoring and control of ethnic violence are outlined in chapter six. These requirements are seen to stem from the generic dynamic structure of the problem presented in chapter four. The predictive inferences provided by the model, are also outlined in this context.

Chapter seven, the last one, focuses on the requirements of a long term steady state solution of the problem. The key factor here is the development of a commonly shared identity for and by the members of different ethnic collectivities. Development of such a super ordinate identity is, however, seen to be realizable only on the durable base of transcendental values. The nature of such a solution, and the means and modes of its implementation, are highlighted. The cascading impact of the solution envisaged here on other intractable social problems,as well as, on the transformation and renewal of a social order, are also delineated. Having taken a look at the objectives and overview of the volume, we now proceed to delineate briefly the situations of ethnic tensions and conflict in Indian and other pluralist societies, in the next chapter.

2

ETHNIC SCHISMS IN INDIAN AND OTHER PLURALIST SOCIETIES

Most of the national societies on the planet today are pluralistic societies. A plural society consists of two or more distinct ethnic groups. An ethnic group is characterized by a high level of the 'consciousness of kind' amongst its members. Consciousness of ethnicity, and ethno-social self-identification, of human beings are related to the bases of their social life. These bases are : caste, community, creed, religion, sect, language, race, region, rituals, sub-culture, symbols, traditions, and common historical experience. Members of an ethnic group define their self-identity in terms of one or more of these social bases. They perceive themselves, and their group, as different from others on the basis of these socio-cultural factor. These factors themselves are the outcomes of long historical process of human dispersal and evolution of man's social institutions and culture. A human being inherits these socio-cultural factors as a consequence of his birth and socialization in an ethnic group. They are internalized in his personality as he grows up and becomes a part of his ethnic community.

INTER-GROUP RELATIONS

Ethnic groups within a pluralistic society may differ from one another in their respective numerical strengths, political orientations, socio-economic affiliations, influence in national affairs, and communal solidarity. Relations between ethnic groups may vary from harmony and complementarity to tension and opprobrium.

Inter-group relations acquire a problem character when they are marked by persisting distrust, tension, disharmony, and conflict. In their problematic form, they vertically divide a plural society from within.

The problem of ethnic schisms and tension is the problem of opprobrious inter-group relations. It is engendered through perceived grievances, deprivations, and non-reciprocated expectations of the ethnic communities towards one another. This perception is usually associated with feelings of distrust, political insecurity, economic disparity and competition, and threats to cultural identity. Such perceptions and feelings have their basis in the social, political, economic, and cultural interests, and aspirations, of the concerned communities. Some of the communal interests and aspirations may derive from the community's heritage of history. The psycho-social schisms emerging in this manner may lead the concerned groups toward intrusive assertions of their respective ethnic differences. Emphasis on ethnic separatism and implicit chauvinism engender the emergence, persistence, and aggravation, of inter- communal tensions.

GRIM CONSEQUENCES AND WIDE-SPREAD NATURE OF ETHNIC SCHISMS

Ethnic conflict in its extreme form is characterized by large scale violence, widespread insurgency, terrorism, rebellion, and civil war. Violence, terrorism, insurgency and war, generate mounting costs of conflict in the form of death, decay, destruction, misery, and suffering of the members of opprobrious groups. A prolonged continuation of such a situation(s) may seriously weaken and disrupt the social order of a pluralistic society, and lead to its politico-economic disintegration.

Conflict amongst ethnic groups is a widely observed social phenomenon across national societies, the world over. Insurgency by Nagas, Mizos, Tripura tribals, and Manipuris, in north-east India; ethnic turbulence in Assam; the Sikh extremism in Punjab; Islamic fundamentalism in Kashmir; middle and scheduled caste tensions in rural areas; and Hindu-Muslim communalism in many parts of the country; are examples of ethno-social conflicts in India. Conflict between the Catholics and Protestants in North Ireland; the Albanians, Croats, and Serbs in Yugoslavia; the Corsicans and the French in Corscica; the Turkish and Greek Cypriots in Cyprus; the Christian and Muslim Arabs in Lebanon; the Sunni Kurds and Shia Muslims in Iran; the Mohajirs and the Sindhis in Pakistan; the Tamils and the Sinhalese in Ceylon; the Muslims and Buddhists in Bangladesh; the whites and the blacks in S. Africa; and the tribal groups in African nations, are some such examples in other plural national socities.

ETHNIC TENSIONS AND CONFLICT IN INDIAN SOCIETY

The problem of ethnic conflict in Indian Society is a very serious one. Internally divisive forces of ethnic separatism are threatening the internal cohesion and territorial integrity of the nation. Frequent recurrence of Hindu-Muslim communal violence in different parts of the country, caste conflicts in the rural areas of several states, insurgency and violence in Nagaland, Manipur, and Tripura, the communal turmoil in Assam, the Sikh extremism in Punjab, the secessionist turbulence in Kashmir, and 'sons of the soil' movement in various regions, define the nature of acute internal schisms in the plural society of India. Although each of these problem situations is historically distinct and unique, they all belong to the generic class of ethno-social conflict in plural societies.

There is thus an imperative need to understand scientifically the complex and dynamic nature of such explosive problem situations. Only through an objective scientific understanding and explanation of this problem-phenomenon, may one be able to find out the necessary and sufficient conditions for controlling the disruptive problem situations.

Indian society is a very large and complex plural society. Its vast population consists of numerous groups and sub-groups that define their identity variously in terms of religion (i.e., Hindus, Muslims, Sikhs, Christians, Jains, etc.), sect (Nirankari, Namdhari and Amritdhari Sikhs, Shia and Sunni Muslims, Hindu denomination groups like Vaishanvites, Lingayats, Shaivites, etc.); language and/or region (Assamese, Bengalis, Gujaratis, Kannadigas, Oriyas, Telgus, etc.), caste (upper, middle, 'backward', and scheduled caste groups), and tribe (Nagas, Mizos, Bodos, Santhals, etc.). They together comprise the richness and variety of social constellations in the social universe of the Indian society.

Pattern of tension and unrest amongst these groups have varied over the years. Some have been chronic and recurrent while others are of more recent origin. Conflict between Hindus and Muslim .. for example, has been chronic. It reached its peak in 1947 with the partition of pre-independence India. Partition was accompanied by killings and uprooting of millions of human beings. Hindu-Muslim conflict has, however, continued even after the partition with recurrent violence. The problem of insurgency in Nagaland and Mizoram on the other hand dates back to the fifties, followed by insurgency in Manipur in the late sixties, and even later in Tripura. Acutely schismatic turbulence in Assam over illegal immigrants from Bangladesh is of more recent origin i.e., from 1979 onward. This simmering situation exploded in February and March 1983, when several thousand persons belonging to tribal groups, immigrant Bengali Muslims, Bengali Hindu immigrants, and native Hindu Assamese were killed, and hundreds of thousands had to flee their lands and homes. This explosion was set off by the elections for state legislature. The problem of Sikh extremism and separatism with its selective violence and terrorism is of yet more recent origin i.e., mainly from 1981 onwards. The problem of Muslim secessionism in Kashmir moved towards insurgency and rebellion in mid-eighties. Conditions leading to emergence of these problems were, however, in the making over much longer periods.

In between the most chronic, and the most recent situations of ethnic tension, are other situations of ethnic schisms. Tensions and violence between the middle and scheduled castes in its current form i.e., a militant assertion of their socio- economic rights by the scheduled castes, and violent reaction of the land owning middle castes in the rural areas, date back to sixties. The crimes against Harijans have, however, a long history. Caste conflicts in Bihar are endemic where all caste groups maintain their armed cadres (*'senas'*). Politics of castes, language, and region, have emerged in the post- independence period as responses of ethnic groups to the dynamics of socio-economic and politico-cultural changes during this period.

ISSUES OF ETHNIC CONFLICTS IN THE INDIAN CONTEXT

Issues characterizing the diverse situations of ethnic conflict in different parts of the country, differ widely. Two common themes underlying them may, however, be discerned. They are the concern of all disaffected groups (i) for the promotion of their sectarian interests, and (ii) the assertion of their distinctive religio-cultural or social identity. Behind these concerns also lies the anxiety of many groups about losing their distinctive cultural symbols, traditions, language, rituals, historical heritage, and 'way of life'. The demands of various groups, and the issues involved in their protests and rebellions. reflect their acute anxiety towards affirming and asserting their distinctive ethno-cultural identities and concerns. Economic and political issues are brought in as supportive elements of the basic underlying themes of resolving the perceived crisis of identity and interests in a milieu of rapid change, increasing competition, and rising aspirations for power and affluence.

Schismatic turbulence in Punjab is centred around the demand for an independent homeland for the Sikhs. For the attainment of this secessionist objective, Sikh extremists have resorted to terrorist violences, kidnappings and murders, bank robberies, ransoms and extortions, derailment of trains, destruction of public property, and massacres of innocent men, women, and children. Their secessionist movement beginning from the early eighties has led to loss of thousands of lives, besides bringing untold misery and suffering to thousands of families. Pakistan and expatriate Sikh organizations provide the extremists with arms, money, and other facilities to wage a continuous war of low intensity against the nation.[1]

Insurgency fomented by fundamentalist Muslim groups in Kashmir,is also centred around the demand for secession from the country. Most of these groups want the valley of Kashmir to become a part of Pakistan. For the attainment of their secessionist objective, they too have to resort to terrorist violence, kidnappings and murders, looting of banks, destruction of public property, coercion, brutalities, and attacks on security personnel. Through their terror tactics, they have also driven out thousands of Hindu families from their homes, and forced them to flee as refugees. Their present intensified phase of rebellion which began from mid-eighties, has so far led to loss of hundreds of lives, besides severely damaging the economy of the state. Pakistan provides the insurgents with sophisticated arms, training, funds, facilities, and sanctuary to wage a continuing war against this country.

Insurgency and terrorism in Assam by extremist Assamese Hindus, are also centred around the demand for an independent homeland. A militant political agitation by Assamese Hindus began in late seventies against the influx of illegal immigrants from Bangla-desh. They perceived serious threats to Assamse language and culture from Bengali domination. They also feared their loss of political power, the loss of control over their state's economic resources of land, oil, tea, and timber, and the pre-empting of economic opportunities as a consequence of the unchecked immigration of 'outsiders' in the state. During this 'anti-foreigner' movement, thousands of people died in inter- ethnic clashes, in various parts of the state, and the economy of the state was immobilized. This movement subsided as the result of a political settlement between the agitating group, and the central government. It, however, soon after, gave way to an extremist underground movement for demanding an independent Assamese state in order to protect the cultural, political, and economic interests of the Assamese Hindu population. The secessionist movement which began in an intensified phase in late eighties, resorted to terrorism, economic blockades, kidnappings, murders, ransom demands, extortions, and attacks on security personnel, for achieving its objective. It also paralysed economic activities in the state, besides leading to loss of hundreds of innocent lives. A military crackdown against the secessionists began in 1991, and resulted in the suppression of their terrorist and disruptive activities.

The nature of a more pervasive and chronic form of ethnic conflict in the country differs from all the three foregoing pattern of schismogenesis. It relates to Hindu-Muslim communal conflicts which have a relatively long history, and continue to occur recurrently in various parts of the country. The communal opprobrium between Hindus and Muslims dates back to the period of British rule and earlier. It led to the partition of the Indian sub-continent in 1947, and has continued to persist in independent India. Unlike the previous three situations, it is not a local or regional problem. As many as 142 districts all over the country have been identified as being prone to 'communal incidents'. Of these, 60 districts have been designated as hyper-sensitive to communal conflict.

Every year scores of violent clashes between Hindus and Muslims occur in diverse parts of the country. Dozens of innocent persons lose their lives in these incidents. Many more are seriously injured and become homeless. Many lose all their meagre possessions besides lives and limbs. The common desideratum in all communal incidents is a collective emotional reaction to supposed hurt and insult to one's religio-communal pride and sentiments in the affected locales. The specific issues of discord precipitating communal conflicts may differ from place to place. They are usually trivial i.e., throwing pieces of meat into religious shrines by mischief makers, dispute over site of a mosque/temple, killing of a cow, loud noise by a procession in front of a mosque, religious conversions, and teasing of a girl of one community by a youth of another community. An underlying background of deep distrust, hate, rage, contempt, and bitterness, however, comes to dominate rapidly the interactions (of persons) of the two communities under the stimuli of perceived 'intolerable' provocation(s) from the 'other side'. Communal organizations and leaders often exploit such situations for promoting their political interests.

Social distance based on mutal avoidance, memories of historical conflicts - old and recent, and chauvinistic religio- cultural exclusivism often characterizes the pattern of inter- group interaction between the Hindus and the Muslim. This pattern of interaction is an outcome of historically rooted negative emotions of the two communal groups toward one another. When random/planned provocations are perceived as serious affronts to its religio-cultural dignity by one or both the communities, these dark and deep emotions surface. If such a situation is tackled in a resolute and timely manner by the local police machinery, these emotions do not amplify and gradually resume their subterranean position with the said incident/event/situation receding into background. If, however, a situation is allowed to deteriorate by reciprocal attempts to 'even-up the score', the emergent emotions amplify rapidly. In their inflamed and amplified state, they lead to mindless perpetration of violence, arson, atrocities, and murders, by the members of the two communities against one another.

The sources of this problem, as mentioned earlier, lie in the deep rooted emotions of distrust, hate, rage, contempt, and bitterness of large sections of the two communities toward each other. These emotions i.e., the affected states are, however, supported by matching cognitive world views of the two communities toward one another. These cognitive world views consist of a set of negative images, beliefs, stereotypes of prejudices about the other community. They are from time to time reinforced by feelings of politco-economic and psycho-cultural insecurities engendered by contemporary socio-political events and developments.

There opprobriuous world views are sociologically interesting in view of the fact that the Muslims of the Indian sub continent are (many generations removed) converts from the native Hindu population of the country.Muslim populace of the country does not constitute a distinct and separate racial stock. Muslim groups differ from region to region in terms of their dress, language, and local customs. They, however, emphasize their groups identity through visible symbols, rituals, and practices, of their common religio-cultural heritage and traditions. They are oriented toward, and identify themselves with, pan-Islamic sentiments and concerns of a world-wide community of Muslims.[2]

Another major form of social schisms and divisiveness is along the lines of castes. Tensions and conflicts between scheduled castes and upper castes, 'backward' castes and scheduled castes, and 'backward' and 'forward' castes, have grown in recent years. Various forms of caste antagonisms in their acute form characterize the social scene in Bihar. A malefic nexus between caste, politics, violence, and crime, has grown throughout the state. Various caste groups have organized themselves politically, and maintain caste'armies' to protect and promote their perceived political and economic interests through a culture of socio-political violence. The tensions and conflicts are "not between the haves and have-nots, but among haves who want to monopolise power and all that goes with it" (Sahay, 1992). In such a situation, violence has become a way of life in Bihar. The role of politicians and criminals often merge together. The rule of law does not exist in various parts of the state (*Ibid*). Caste tensions in their latent, as well as, overt form, are also present in most parts of the country.

The movement of various tribal groups in the country, represent another form and dimension of ethnic cleavages in the country. The Gorkhaland agitation in West Bengal, Jharkhand movement in Bihar, Bodoland agitation in Assam, and tribal insurgency in Tripura, Manipur, and Nagaland, are primarily ethno-political in nature. Their potential for ethnic tension and conflict, however, stems from their focus against 'outsiders'/'foreigners' on the one hand, and recourse to opprobrious violence on the other. They lead the non-tribals to organize and arm themselves for their safety, or leave the affected areas. The capacity and willingness of the government to protect them is perceived as weak.

Issues of ethnic conflicts in Indian society thus show both apparent similarities and dissimilarities. They all, however, represent complex configurations of ethno-cultural, economic, political, and socio-religious issues. Mutual distrust and tensions among the social groups involved is their foremost common feature. All of them are also characterized by varying degrees of violence and disruption.

ISSUES OF ETHNIC CONFLICT IN OTHER PLURALIST SOCIETIES

Ethnic conflicts in other pluralist societies are also characterized by the disaffected groups' deep concern for the preservation and assertion of their cultural identities. This concern is also underlaid by perceived economic grievances. political insecurity, and demographic pressures. Economic discrimination and perceived lack of economic, political,and educational opportunities are major issues of discord in North Ireland, Yugoslavia, Corsica and Cyprus. Economic despair, political deprivation, and ethno-cultural aspirations, are the focal issues behind the secessionist rebellions of Kurds in Iran, Iraq and Turkey; Tamils in Sri Lanka; Turks in Cyprus; Arabs in Israel; and tribal groups in African nations. In many cases of ethnic conflict in pluralistic societies, the situations have been complicated and worsened by the involvement of external forces in the internal schisms.

Situations of ethnic tensions and conflicts do not emerge suddenly. Each situation is distinguished by its ante cedent causal and contributory factors which may have had their origins in history and/or in contemporary events. In Sri Lanka, a small plural society, for example, the present bitter civil war between the Tamils and the Sinhalese began in early eighties. The schismatic situation has, however, been in the making since the early fifties soon after the country's freedom from the British rule.

Tamils and Sinhalese differ from one another in language, culture, religion, and ethnic origin. During the period of British rule, Tamils were able to progress more in the fields of education, bureaucracy, professions, trade, industry, and commerce. After independence, this primacy was systematically ended by the Sri Lankan Government. The communal chauvinism of Sinhalese politicians, the politics of Buddhist revivalism, growing lack of opportunities for the Tamil youth, discriminatory measures against the Tamils and their language, and recurrent anti–Tamil riots from 1956 onward, together, escalated the grievances and opprobrium of Tamils, and led them first to demand political automony, and later to the demand for an independent Tamil State. The situation has gradually graduated from political agitations and protests by Tamils to their recourse to terrorism, insurgency, and civil war. Over the years, thousands of lives have been lost, towns have been destroyed, hundreds of thousands have become homeless, and fled as refugees. This intensely violent conflict is, however, still continuing (1992).

In Lebanon, another small but highly complex pluralistic society, thousands of innocent men, women, and children have died in a grim multi-lateral ethnic conflict involving Christian and Muslim Arabs, the Druze population, the Israelites, the Palestinians, and the Syrians. The population, of the small nation which came into existence in 1920, is almost equally divided between Christians and Muslims. An institutionalised system of political accommodation between the two communities enabled the country to develop peacefully for years. External changes beginning in the fifties and involving the emergency of pan-Arab nationalist ideology, influx of a large number of armed Palestinians making terrorist attacks on Israel from Lebanese territory, Israel's retaliatory raids inside Lebanon dislocating its economy, and the stationing of Syrian troops in the country, were some of the developments that destroyed the country's communal peace and polarised its population. Arab Christians, who owned most of the industry and trade in the country, wanted the Palestinians to leave the country, while Muslim Arabs felt morally bound to support the Palestinian cause.

The Lebanese Christians supported by Israel, and Arab Muslim factions supported by Iran and Syria, fought a bitter civil war for years, which left the country in ruins. Western countries and Syria were able to establish peace of a sort only in 1991, by disarming the various armed groups engaged in conflict after a long and costly military effort.

In Nigeria, a relatively large pluralistic society, tribal schisms began to grow between the majority tribe of Hausa Fulani and the minority tribe of Ibos, in the sixties soon after the country's independence from British rule. Hausa Fulani, contituting more than half of the country's population are Muslims, and live in the northern and central part of the country. Ibos, constituting less than one fourth of the population, are Christians, and live in the southern part of the country. They are also the most educated, and relatively more advanced of all the tribal groups in the country. They dominated the country's administration, professions, and services. This dominance was resented by the Hausa Fulani, who wanted to assert their primacy over the affairs the newly independent nation. When the Government, and the army, dominated by them began to initiate moves and measures against the interests of Ibos, tensions between the two groups intensified leading to large scale riots, military coups, murders of political figures, disturbances, and economic blockades.

This situation exploded into a bitter civil war in the seventies with the Ibos proclaiming their independence, and establishing their own state of Biafra. After years of bitter civil war, in which tens of thousands of people died in fighting and mass starvation, Ibos were defeated. A military government representing a form of accommodation between various tribal groups, has been managing the country's affairs since then. Tensions, schisms, and disintegrative tendencies on the one hand, and corruption and maladministration on the other, characterize the nation's contemporary socio-political scene.

Each situation of opprobrium between ethnic groups within and across societies, is a historic individualism. It is also differentiated from other analogous situations in terms of its social actors, groups, cultural bases, economic issues, political discords, nature and forms of opprobrium, and the level and modes of violence. All of them, however, display certain similar types of feature and characteristics. They are outlined next.

COMMON CHARACTERISTICS OF ETHNIC CONFLICT SITUATIONS

Opprobrium between ethnic groups is a form of conflict over their perceived cultural, economic, and political interest and aspirations. This form of conflict may be seen to be characteried by a set of its distinctive defining characteristics.These characteristics are definable in diverse situations of ethnic conflict across space and time. They may briefly be outlined as follows:

[1] The first and perhaps the most basic characteristic of such situations is the perceived ethnic basis of their self-identity by members of the ethnic groups. The *'consciousness of kind'* involved in such a mode of collective perception sets the members of a group apart from other people. The group members view themselves as 'different' from others in terms of their distinctive socio-cultural attributes and define their identity accordingly.

[II] Another characteristic logically related to the first is the presence of communal organizations for the affirmation of the groups's distinctive socio-cultural identity, and the promotion of group members' collective interests. These organizations elicit the loyalty and commitment of the group members. They play a major role in guiding the groups' affairs, and determining its collective responses to extant and emerging situations facing the community.

[III] Another major observable charcteristic is the strongly sectarian socio-political orientation of members of the ethnic groups in conflict. This characteristic is a logical extension of the first two in conjunction. This leads the group members to view and adjudge every issue, event, or situation, from the circumscribed perspective of their narrow sectarian group interests.

[IV] Ethnic groups in conflicts are also characterized by their respective perceived grievances and sense of deprivation. The grievances may pertain to economic, political, or socio-cultural issues/events/situations. They tend to amplify as a consequence of economic and demographic pressures experienced by one or both the groups.

[V] Organized political expression of sectarian demands for the perceived protection or promotion of group interests is another distinctive characterizing feature of the situation. The demands may range from securing exclusive economic and political benefits for the group, to autonomy, secession and independence.

[VI] The preceding characteristic generates another distinguishing feature of the situation in the form of the opprobrious reaction of the other group(s) to the sectarian demands of one group. It is this aspect of the situation that provides momentum to the escalation of inter-group conflict.

[VII] The confrontation between sectarian demands of the two groups, or the opprobrious reaction of the other group to the demands of its opposing group, generates and amplifies mutual distrust and tensions between the two groups. Each group comes to believe that its 'legitimate' objectives and interests can be met only at the cost of the other group. Their definition of the situation acquires the form of a *zero-sum game.*

[VIII] Amplifying mutual distrust and tensions, and the zero-sum definition of the situation by one or both the groups, leads to induction of violence in the opprobrious state of affairs. The spectrum of violence may range from communal riots and terrorism to murders, massacres, and civil war. The terrorist activities may include destruction of public and private property, kidnappings, extortions, intimidation, torture, ransom demands, and looting of public funds, besides purposive as well as, mindless insensate violence against innocent civilians. This overt,highly visible, and most grievious feature of the conflict situation may broadly be characterized as disturbed law and order conditions.

[IX] Disturbed law and order conditions are highly correlated with the armed action by the Government of the country to cope with these conditions. The Government action may include deployment of security personnel for checking, seeking, and destroying the men and material of the group(s) engaged in disruptive activities, terrorism and insurgency.

[X] Another distinctive feature of the conflict situations is the cost of conflict incurred by the opposing sides. This cost is usually high in terms of the loss of life and resources. It is however, incomputable in terms of human misery and suffering. Escalating cost of conflict may also generate pressures toward resolving the discords.

[XI] Policies and responses of the country's government toward dealing with the conflict situation, is another common feature. The policies and responses may range from seeking the problem's solution on the basis of negotiation/reconcilitation, to the determined suppression of terrorism, rebellion, insurgency by forçe. The nature of a goverment's policies and responses are determined by its own political interests and compulsions.

[XII] Many, though not all situtions of ethnic conflict, are also characterized by the involvement of external agencies and powers. the latter may extend help to a disaffected group in the form of arms, money, training, and sanctuary. Such help is usually provided by external entities to promote their own political obectives and interests.

The foregoing empirically observable characteristics of ethnic conflict situations are not, however, their discrete and unrelated elements. They are, on the other hand, inter-related together in a multi-lateral manner. This inter-relationship amongst them serves to define the generic dynamic structure of this class of conflict situations. Such a dynamic structure is developed and elucidated in chapter four.

This chapter has outlined the nature and dimensions of ethnic conflicts in Indian and other pluralistic societies. As mentioned earlier, terrorist activities and violence represent a very grim aspect of many such situations Such is certainly the case in respect of the turbulent schisms in Kashmir, Punjab, and Assam (1992). The psycho-social nature and bases of the phenomenon of terrorism are explicated in the next chapter.

Reference

1. See Appendix I.
2. See Appendix II.

3

THE NATURE AND FUNCTIONS OF TERRORISM

The grim and brutal phenomenon of terrorist violence may be related to inter-group and/or political conflicts. In the present context, we are, however, primarily concerned with the graduation of inter-communal tensions toward terrorist violence and insurgency. In most of such situations, struggle for political power, is also an integral and crucial part of the turbulent scenarios of hate, rage, violence, and schisms.

WHAT IS TERRORISM?

Terrorism is a disorderly violent psycho-political phenomenon observable in many parts of the globe.[1] Bangladesh, Burma, India, Pakistan, Phillipines, and Sri Lanka, in South and South- East Asia; Cyprus, Iraq, Israel, Lebanon, Turkey, Yemen, and UAE in Middle Asia; Angola, Egypt, Ethiopia, Mozambique, Nigeria, Somalia, Sudan, South Africa, Uganda, Zaire, and Zimbabwe, in Africa; El-Salvador, Nicaragua, Costa Rica, and Haiti in Central America; Bolivia, Chile, Argentina, Colombia, Peru, Surinam, and Venezuela, in South America; and Corsica, Italy, North Ireland, Sardinia, Spain, and Yugoslavia, in Europe have been seriously beset with this problem-phenomenon. The list of nations given above is by no means exhaustive. The nature, context, and magnitude, of terrorist activities in these nations differ widely. They may range from sporadic acts of violence and destruction to organized insurgency and rebellions.

Terrorism is organized political violence designed to deter opposition by maximising fear. Execution of randomly timed violent acts by the members of a terrorist group is the main part of their political strategy for achieving their ethno-political objectives. This strategy seeks to create terror in order to as Trotsky (1961) put it, 'break the will of class enemies' to resist. Ghastly violence against innocent civilians, planned murders, crude intimidation, dacoities, hostage taking, kidnapping, plane hijackings, sacrilege of holy places, bomb and grenade attacks on public places and persons, and attacks on diplomatic missions, are some of the activities carried out by terrorist groups as part of their sustained political campaign of organized violence.

The foregoing and similar acts are designed to deter opposition by maximising the latter's fear. The acts involve planned, as well as, random targetting of people and sites in order to enhance their impact and surprise value. The more insecure and vulnerable can a people be made to feel, the more likely would they be to concede the group's political demands. A major overall objective is to convince the Government personnel and others that any appearance of opposition on their part will lead to severely damaging consequences. Terrorization aims not only at 'eliminating' and neutralizing specific opponents (which in the present context are designated as 'anti-Panth'/'anti-Assamese'/'anti-Kaum') but also to show that the cost of opposition would be unacceptably high to those daring to oppose. Terrorism may thus be characterized as methodical violence intended to deter actual and potential opposition to the groups' political demands. In this sense, terrorism is also a form of communication intended to shape the public opinion (Schmid and DeGraaf, 1982).

TERRORIST ACTIVITIES

In order to accomplish their perceived socio-political objectives, the terrorists usually engage in the following types of activities (Rastogi, 1988):

I. Killings for terror which include massacres of bus and train passengers, and bomb and grenade attacks on civilians in markets, railway station, cinema houses, and public gatherings.

II. Looting of public funds from banks and organizations.

III. Destructive activities which may include hijacking of planes, burning of bridges and buildings, derailment of trains, desecration of holy places, and destruction of public and private property.

IV. Intimidation, extortion, and kidnappings of businessmen, officials, security personnel, or their family members for ransom, blackmail, or coercion.

V. Assasinations of public figures, and perceived opponents including 'informers'.

VI. Attacks on police patrols, outposts, and armouries, and

VII. Murders of security personnel and/or their family members.

The overall purpose and rationale of these activities is to create an overpowering climate of terror, and an acute sense of insecurity among the perceived opponents of the terrorists' aims and objectives. Persistant reluctance and refusal of public willingness to come forward, and identify the terrorists in numerous cases of daylight murders, and bank robberies, attest to the extremists' success in creating terror and deterrence. Witnesses are warned that if they assist the police, they and their families would be wiped out. Murders of security personnel and their family members, and the failure of authorities to apprehend the murderers, serve to reinforce the threats and warnings of the terrorists. 'Success' of the extremists in turn, serve to weaken the will and morale of the law-enforcement personnel. The climate of terror, violence, threats, and insecurity, also ensures people's conformity with the obedience to the terrorists calls for frequent *bandhs* (general strike) and 'people's curfew', to demonstrate their power and hold over the people.

ENABLING CONDITIONS OF TERRORIST ACTIVITIES

Emergence, growth, and persistence of the terrorists' acts of violence and intimidation depend on the presence of certain prerequisites enabling the terrorists to engage in organized violence. These enabling conditions may be listed as follows (Rastogi,1988):

I. Availability of arms, expertise, and arms training to the terrorists.

II. Availability of money and other infra-structural resources to them.

III. Availability of safe hideouts and sanctuaries to them.

IV. Easy escape after crimes.

V. Availability of sensitive intelligence about targets, and security operations, to them from their sympathisers and collaborators in Government agencies.

VI. Availability of indoctrinated youths as terrorist recruits.

VII. Covert organizational set up with supportive linkages to political front organizations.

VIII. Terrorization of public.

IX. Inadequate or weak security apparatus.

X. Nexus of terrorists with smugglers, drug traffickers and arms merchants.

XI. Propagation of religio-political or ethno-centred ideology of hate and separatism.

XII. Active support of a section of the ethnic community to terrorists, including ex-Servicemen and police personnel.

XIII. Control of terrorists over the management and resources to community's public places.

XIV. Restraints placed on the operations of security personnel.

These enabling conditions are primarily concerned with the availability to terrorists of money, arms, training, cultural communication channels for group mobilization, secure bases of operation, fanatical leadership, indoctrinated cadres, and so on. Financial resources are often available to terrorist groups from external sources besides funds obtained through lootings of banks, ransoms from kidnappings, and contributions from sympathisers. These enabling conditions together provide the base for the superstructure of terrorist groups and their activities. Terrorist operatives also rely upon the support and sympathy of some sections of their own community toward their cause and programme of actions.

SOCIOLOGICAL CONDITIONS

Sociologically, two major conditions must be present in conjunction to engender the emergence of terrorism and terrorists as a socio-political phenomenon.

I. One important condition is a group's perception of its conflict with other group(s) as zero-sum. The group believes that its gain can occur only at the cost of the other group's loss. The demand for an independent homeland for the Sikhs is clearly of this type i.e., it can be realized only at the cost of the Hindus of Punjab. The demand for the detection, disfranchisement and deportation of the 'foreigners' in Assam is also of a zero-sum nature. So is the demand of Kashmiri militants for separation from the country.

II. Another sociological condition refers to the presence of a self-sufficient sectarian culture, and a group-centred ideology, predicated around the primacy of communal interests and values. When the ideology and culture also justify the use of violence for sectional goals, an important stimulus for group violence exists. The Sikhs as a community conform to this condition and so do the Assamese, and Kashmiri extremists.

These sociological conditions, however, need to be understood in the context of the psychology of the terrorists. Without an insight into the nature of the mental make up of the terrorists, the significance of the sociological conditions, cannot be properly appreciated.

THE PSYCHOLOGY OF TERRORISTS

Terrorists view the world in absolute polar terms of good *vs.* evil, and us *vs.* them. Compromise and accommodations are ruled out by the extreme and stark nature of their ideological stand-point. They are highly rigid in their outlook, and prone toward risk in their actions.

The fanaticism of terrorists serves to overcome their feelings of guilt, emptiness, alienation, and depression. Their fanaticism also leads them to lose sight of reality. They come to believe their own propaganda and in the imminence of their victory. They thence tend to over estimate their strength, public appeal, and weakness of their enemies.

As terrorism continues over a prolonged period without achieving its political goals, the terrorist activity acquires the character of common crimes. But for a thin political cover, the operations of terrorist group(s) come to resemble those of ordinary criminal gangs.

Terrorists hold absolute and unquestionable convictions about political problems and issues. These convictions enable them to give a subjective moral justification to their otherwise cruel and evil acts of brutality, and violence. The sensitivity of terrorists toward the moral rights of their victims as human beings, is deadened by their fanatic indoctrination and outlook.

Terrorist violence serves both *instrumental* and *expressive* purposes. It is action toward realizing their vision, and the latter serves to protect them from guilt feelings. The violence also serves to strengthen the solidarity of the group in terms of shared risks, dangers and thrills. Aggression and violence also serve to aggrandize their egos and generate in them what Sorel calls 'sentiments of glory'.

A terrorist's a self-image is that of a dedicated and brave soldier fighting for a noble and glorious cause. This is reflected in the speeches and writings of their leaders. It is also brought out in their demands to be treated as prisoners of war when captured by security personnel.

Participation in terrorist activities also meets the youths' powerful idealistic urge to devote their lives for a cause, a leader, and an ideology. This urge is a part of the broader human urge for seeking meaning and purpose in life. The charismatic leadership of Bhindranwale, the vision of establishing *Khalsa* supremacy, and the ideology of militant religio-political revivalism, provide Sikh extremists with emotional fulfilment. This type of warped psychological hold on the minds of credulous masses is, however, not something new. It has historically been observed in the youth bands of Nazi Germany, Fascist Italy, Imperialist Japan, and Khomani's Iran.

BELIEF SYSTEM OF TERRORISTS

Terrorists, the world over have been seen to hold certain common beliefs (Hazelip, 1980). The world-view of a terrorist as a social role type appears to consist of a distinctive set of cognitive elements. These cognitive elements i.e., beliefs may be outlined as follows:

(i) Use of violence is imperative for over-throwing tyranny and oppression.

(ii) The scope of violence against 'the enemy'is unlimited.

(iii) A terrorist act must clearly express its purpose, and convey a telling message to the parties concerned. The major purpose of acts is to eliminate/neutralize the enemy and the message is to deter the opposition.

(iv) Uncompromising ruthlessness in the execution of terrorist missions is essential for the success of their cause.

(v) Frequency of attacks, selection of targets, and scope and level of violence and destruction, should be such as to break the enemy's will and incapacitate its operations.

(vi) Secrecy is of vital importance in carrying out terrorist missions.

(vii) Failures, ineffectiveness and inefficiency of the government may be used to increase the peoples' support for their cause and the group, and

(viii) Ones' firmness of ideological convictions should be matched by his operational flexibility in the use of violence as the exclusive instrument.

The foregoing elements of the terrorists' belief system are also borne out by the nature and pattern of the terrorist operations in Assam, Kashmir, and Punjab. The Sikh, Kashmiri and Assamese terrorists are no exceptions in this respect. The elements of the terrorist belief system also bring out the inevitable and unavoidable role of short term control measures involving the government's armed action. They also indicate the difficult and long term nature of the communication process aiming at change in the actors' rigid subjective world views. The latter are strongly characterized by pathological learning, self- closure, and impermeability. Increasing the costs of conflict, for them appears to be the first essential pre-requisite for softening the rigidity of the terrorists' mental make-up. Only then, may the emissions of communication stimuli toward inter group peace and harmony may register on their mind.

References

1. For a further and more detailed discussion of terrorism as a psycho-political phenomenon, see, Devine and Rafalko (1982), Fromkin (1975), Hazelip (1980), Jenkins (1982), Trotsky (1961) and Turk (1982) among others.

4

DYNAMICS OF ETHNIC CONFLICT SITUATIONS[1]

The problem of inter-communal tension is a complex dynamic social phenomenon. It requires a multi-cyclical structure for its representation. Development of a multi-cyclical structure is based on an integrative approach. Multi-disciplinary knowledge, relevant information from diverse sources, and a wide variety of empirical evidence, are assembled in the form of inter-related propositions. The latter form the basis for the identification of variables and their relationships. The variables, and their relationships, are then organized in the form of inter-acting feed back cycles. In what follows, the process of developing the problem's dynamic structure is illustrated briefly. The structure is meant to codify all the relevant knowledge and information available to the analyst. It is subject to validation on the scientific criteria of economy of concepts, internal non-contradiction, and compatibility with empirical evidence. The model's ability to generate the past, present, and future modes of variation of the phenomenon, is crucial. The model has to be empirically sustainable and verifiable. It has to be moreover, transcultural, i.e., applicable to situations of ethnic conflict across space and time. In this manner, the isomorphism of ethnic conflict situations can be brought out.

ETHNIC SELF-IDENTIFICATION AND ITS RE-INFORCEMENT

The starting points in the present context are the socialization, and life-experiences of the individuals, that impel them towards their self-identification as members of a particular ethnic group. Socialization and life-experiences provide the powerful socio-cultural inputs (caste, community, language, symbols, religion, rituals, race, and region, etc.) on the basis of which individuals define their ethnic social position. The latter then engenders attitudes, beliefs, and perception of interests, corresponding to ethnic self-identification. This follows from the basic theorem of the sociology of knowledge. According to this theorem, the subjective mental world views (*weltanschauung*) of the individuals are based on the social bases of their existence (Durkheim and Mauss, 1901-2; Mannheim, 1936). The strength of ethnic attitudes, beliefs, and interests, leads the individuals toward empathy with, and participation in the ethnic collectivities. The ethnic organizations and media serve to affirm the socio-cultural identity of their members and promote their interests on the basis of shared concerns and mutual help. Such a participative experience then serves to reinforce the individuals' self-identification with their ethnic group.

The foregoing set of propositions and their inter-relationships are representable in the form of a feed back cycle as follows:

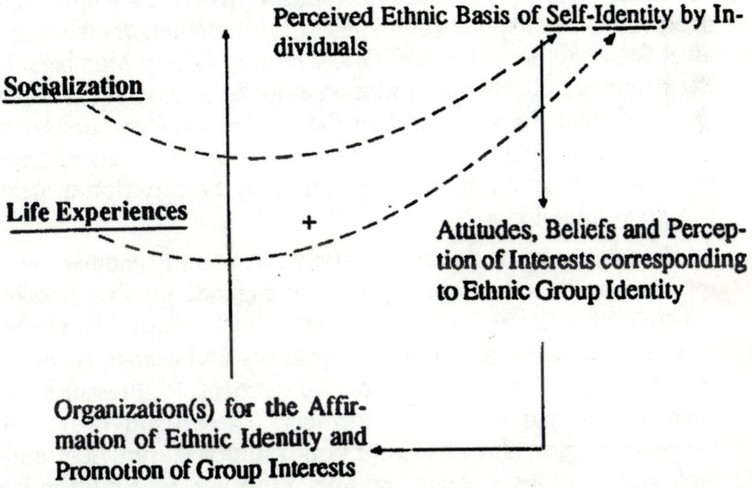

Fig. 1. Re-inforcement of the ethnic basis of self-identification by individuals

Figure 1 shows a positive feed back cycle. It depicts a process that reinforces the individual's definition of their ethnic identity. Socialization, and life experiences, are here analytically shown as exogenous variables. The variables not included within a system cycle are deemed as exogenous. This distinction in many cases is however, for analytic convenience only. In a larger model for example, where these two variables may be shown to be affected over a long period by operation of universalistic processes of secular education and modernization, they would cease to be exogenous.

Now, if on the plane of social values, we regard the ethnic basis of social identification as 'bad', then this cycle is malfunctioning. On the other hand, if we adopt the perspective of cultural pluralism, and the individuals' right to preserve and develop their socio-cultural heritage, then this cycle is deemed to be operating normally as long as the promotion of particular interests does not lead to an abrassive and/or chauvinistic parochialism. Whether, or not, such an ethnic exclusivism develops amongst the group members would depend on a set of political, historicals, and economic factors. These factors would, however, be empirically observable. This aspect of ethnic exclusivism defines another variable, Sectarian Socio-Political Orientation of Group Members. If the ethnic organization(s), and media, foster a sense of exclusive and parochial chauvinism, then the group members' Sectarian Socio-Political Orientation would be evidenced as casteism/communalism/regionalism, etc., depending on the empirical context of a given situation.

Surveying contemporary situations, we identify another starting point as the universalistic processes engendering Pressures of Socio-Political Change and Modernization including industrialism and urbanism. The pressures of modernity and change generate corresponding Requirements of Adjustment to Pressures of Change on the part of the group members. These requirements call for psychological change toward non-traditional and wider outlook and attitudes. Change attempts, however, encounter resistance and inertia from pre-existing attitudes and beliefs of individuals defining their identity and interests in traditional and/or narrow ethnic terms.

PSYCHOLOGICAL CRISES AND SECTARIANISM

Pursuit of perceived political and economic interests by the group members under conditions of modernity and change thus leads them to the psychological crises of identity and insecurity. These anxiety-laden psychological crises are then sought to be met through the social anchorages of ethnic collectivities and communal solidarity. The resultant bonds of emotional affiliation and perceived interests, produce and strengthen the Sectarian Socio-Political Orientation of Group Members. Such an orientation (i.e.. casteism/communalism/regionalism) thence serve to resolve the group members' Problems of Identity, Insecurity and Politico-Economic Interests. The phenomenon of casteism/communalism/regionalism, and other forms of ethnic parochialism, are thence seen to serve the function of enabling the members of an ethnic group to adjust to the conditions of social change in terms of their traditional social moorings and definition of identity.

Modernization mobilizes ethnic groups and converts them into active politico-cultural collectivities (Rothschild, 1981). Rapidity of social change and non-traditional values engendered by modernization, generate feelings of alienation, loss of direction, and emotional insecurity, in the individuals subjected to pressures of change. They consequently seek to affirm their social identities by strengthening their commitment to the religio – cultural values of their ethnic communities. Modernization also often leads to an uneven re-distribution of economic and political resources amongst the ethnic groups. This also promotes their Sectarian Socio-Political Orientation for the purposes of maintaining, and/or improving, their politico- economic position.

The representation of the cyclic feed back processes involved here may be outlined as in Figure 2.

Figure 2 shows the inter-action of three feed back cycles, one positive and two negative. Cycle 1 discussed earlier, is here encompassed within the orbit of cycle 2. Cycle 2 inter-relates together the variables, Problems of Identity, Insecurity and Politico-Economic Interests (for the group members); Organization(s) for the Affirmation of Ethnic Identity and Promotion of Group Interests; Perceived Ethnic Basis of self-identity by individuals; and Attitudes, Beliefs and Perceptions of Interests Corresponding to Ethnic Group Identity. It is a negative feedback cycle. It aims at meeting

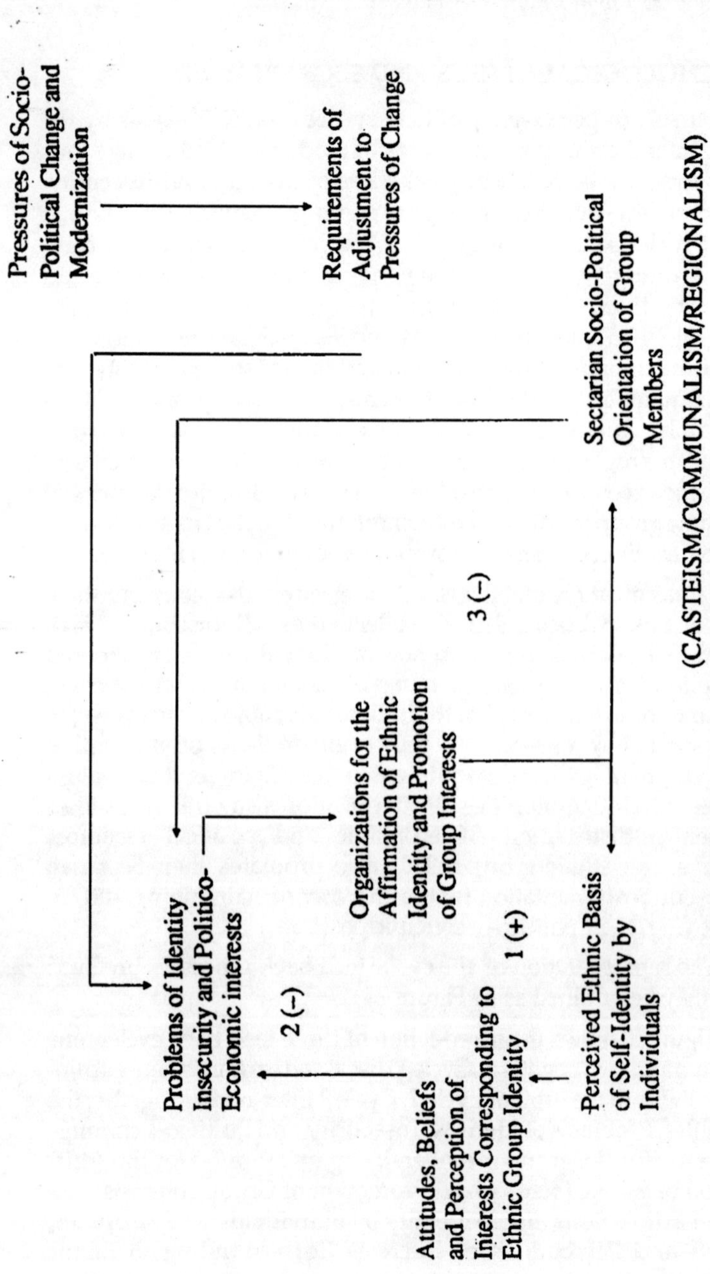

Fig. 2. Psycho-social basis of ethnic sectarianism

the problems of identity, insecurity and interests of group members through their empathic participation in sectarian organization(s) for the affirmation of their ethnic identity and promotion of particular interests.

Cycle 3 inter-relates together the variables, Problems of Identity, Insecurity and Politico-Economic Interests; Organization(s) for the Affirmation of Ethnic Identity and Promotion of Group Interests; and Sectarian Socio-Political Orientation of Group Members. It is also a negative feedback cycle. It aims at meeting the problems of identity, insecurity and interests through the sectarian socio-political orientation and behaviour of the ethnic group members. It is this aspect of the phenomenon of inter-ethnic relations that is visible in the form of casteism/communalism/regionalism, etc., i.e., the exclusivist behaviour pattern of the members of an ethnic group.

In figure 2, the variable, Organization(s) for the Affirmation of Ethnic Identity and Promotion of Group Interests, stands at the intersection of all the three feed back cycles. It is as such the most *salient* variable in the above three cycles.

Both the cycles 2 and 3 may here be viewed as malfunctioning, in so far as, the requirements of adjustment to modernity and change of the ethnic group members are seen to be met through their inculcation of parochial socio-political orientation and responses. This aspect of the situation attests variously to the absence, ineffectiveness, and failure, of the universal institutions of the larger society to harmoniously integrate the members of an ethnic group on the basis of a supra- ethnic set of social values.

EMERGENCE AND GROWTH OF TENSIONS

The foregoing institutional failure leads to a persistence of the problems of identity, insecurity, and interests, of the ethnic group on the one hand, and their exclusivist socio- political orientation on the other. When these problems and orientation are further aggravated by the economic difficulties of inflation and unemployment[2] on the one hand, and a disharmonious heritage of recent and past history on the other, a collective sense of Perceived Grievances and Deprivation of Ethnic Group Members, emerges. Such a collective perception then finds organized political expression in the form of sectional demands and protests. The background of ethnic organizations and media aids the group's political mobilization. The organized Political Expression of Sectarian Demands, and protests may also be variously amplified (random) exogenously by the group's leadership and resources, internal factionalism, geographic position, and the support of external agencies[3]. The nature of demands and protests in turn, however, affect the perception and Reactions of Other (ethnic) Group(s). The inter-action of demands and protests of one group with the perception and reactions of the other group(s), serves to generate Mutual Distrust and Tension. Mutual Distrust and Tensions, thence, serve to reinforce the Perceived Deprivation and Grievances of Ethnic Group Members. The high values of the distrust and tension variable brought about by random/planned provocative acts of extremists, may give rise to Disturbed Law and Order Conditions. The latter may take the form of emotionally charged demonstrations, riots, arson and violence. Persisting high values of this variable are evidenced by insurgency, terrorism, and civil war. Disturbed conditions call forth the Government's Armed Action to deal with the violent opprobrium of groups.

The circular reactive processes involved in the foregoing discussion may be depicted as in fig. 3.

Figure 3 shows the self-reinforcing (i.e., the positive feed back) nature of the process of ethnic tension. The nature of the variables and their relationships have been discussed earlier. The relationship between the variables, Disturbed Law and Order Conditions, and Government's Armed Action denotes a negative feed back cycle whose intended regulatory role is to control riotous conditions by armed action. Frightening experiences of individuals caught up in the turmoil of Disturbed Law and Order Conditions, however, become a lasting part of their Life Experiences. The latter then serve to strengthen the Perceived Ethnic Basis of Self-Identity by Individuals.

COSTS OF CONFLICT AND GOVERNMENT POLICIES

Analysing the phenomenon further, one finds that the loss of life and property caused by violent disturbances, represent the Costs of Conflict for the rival communities and the Government. The magnitude of disturbed conditions and the costs of conflict are also affected by the resources of arms and organized manpower

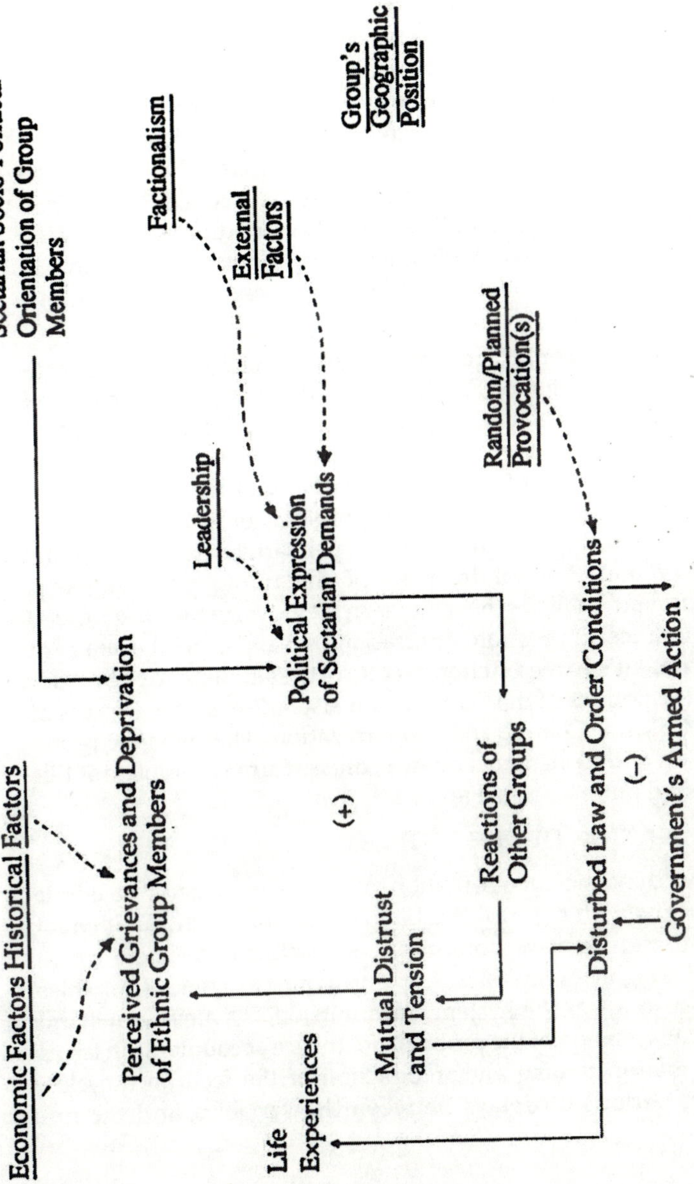

Fig. 3. Self-re-inforcing nature of the process of ethnic tension

used by the opprobrious groups in their conflict. The expenditure incurred by the Government in deploying large number of armed personnel to deal with terrorists, insurgents, and rioters; the injuries and loss of life suffered by security men; damage to public property, and loss of production and revenue due to restraints on economic activities; generate costs of conflict for theGovernment. The costs of conflict for the ethnic groups include loss of life and limbs, destruction of property and possessions; adverse effect on the students' careers; economic losses sustained by traders, businessmen and industrialists; starvation conditions faced by the poor due to absence of work and wages; and the tragedies due to non-availability of medicines and medical care owing to curfew, *bandhs*, and so on.

The costs of conflict go to affect the sense of Perceived Grievances and Deprivation of Ethnic Group Members, the Reactions of Other (Ethnic) Group(s) and the Government's Assessment of Political Implications of the communal conflict. Government's Assessment of Political Implications, determines the Government's Policies for dealing with the problem of ethnic tensions. Government's Policies are; however, primarily determined by the Ideology and Political Interests of the ruling political party. Government's policies thence govern the Goverment's response(s) to the Political Expression of Sectarian Demands, and the nature of Government's Armed Action to control the situation. At a broader level, the policies of the Government also influence the Process of Socio-Cultural Change and Modernization. The dynamic representation of the phenomenon in a concise form is complete at this point, and outlined as in Figure 4.

EXPLANATION OF THE PROBLEM

The dynamic representation of the phenomenon of ethnic tension given in Figure 4 is seen to consist of seventeen interact positive and negative non-linear feedback cycles. These cycles comprise eighteen variables. As many as nine exogenous variables are seen to affect the system from outside[4]. Diverse forms and modes of variation of the problem are thence accountable in terms of the malfunctioning and inter-action of the feed back cycles, varying periods of delays between the variables, and the im-

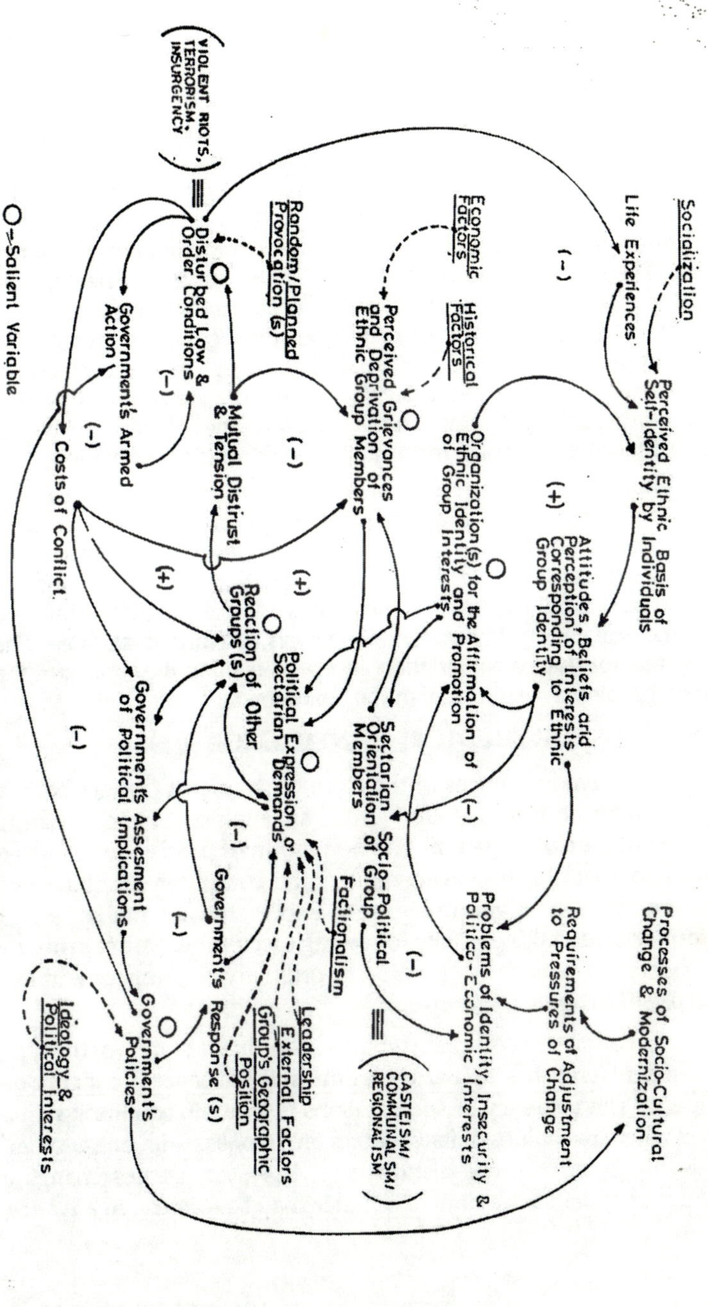

FIG. 4: DYNAMICS OF ETHNIC TENSION IN SOCIETIES

pacts of exogenous variables on the internal dynamics of a given problem situation.

The explanation of the problem is provided by the latter's dynamic multi-cyclical structure. The nature and number of internal and external variables, the specification of their forms and modes of inter action with other variables, their sequential and cyclic organization into interacting feed back cycles, and the identification of the cycles polarities, together comprise the explanatory base. The variables of the system cognize the subjective perception, attitudes, beliefs, and images, of the social actors involved in the problem, as well as, the objective politico-economic factors and environmental conditions associated with the problem situation. They, thence, provide an integrated and time varying picture of a given problem situation when mapped onto the actors, issue events, collectivities, space and time of that specific empirical situation.

Explanation and prediction are symmetrically related. Predictive inferences in the proper sense of the term (as distinct from projections and trend extrapolations) cannot be derived in the absence of a theoretical understanding and explanation of the phenomenon concerned. Similarly, in the absence of verifiable predictive inferences, the explanatory framework of analysis, remains invalidated. The inter relationship of explanation and prediction in the context of the given problem is explicated in the next section.

ANALYSIS FOR PREDICTIVE INFERENCE

Predictive inferences of the form, 'If X, then Y' where both X and Y may be plural, follow from an analysis of the dynamic representation of a system. The derivation of precise quantitative inferences would, however, require the computer simulation of system model as given in Figure 4. This is, however, a large and complex undertaking. In the following discussion, we are primarily concerned with the derivation of predictive inferences without the use of a digital computer.

The course of a complex dynamic non-linear system of the type given here tends to stabilize over time in the absence of exogenous impacts. The tendency of such systems is to attain equilibrium at a level where the values of its variables are in phase with one another. The impact of external disturbances, however, creates changing modes of system behaviour. The latter may be foreseen in advance, and subsequently, compared with empirical observations of system behaviour during the relevant period. Three complementary modes of predictive inference may in this context be identified as follows:

I. Inferences regarding the state and course of a system as a consequence of the exogenous impacts on specific system variables.

II. Inferences regarding the state and course of a system as a result of changes in the system's endogenous controllable variables, and

III. Inferences regarding the contemporaneous values of a system's remaining salient variables on the basis of an empirical estimation of the values of any one or a few salient variables.

These three modes of predictive inferences may be combined together for a more adequate analysis.

Predictive inferences for the given system in mode I (i.e., impact of exogenous factors) may be illustrated as follows:

(1) As long as the environments of the children in family, clan, school, and neighbourhood (i.e., socialization) continue to rigorously emphasize the religio-cultural traditions and exclusivism of their ethnic group(s), they would grow up perceiving their identity and social interests in narrow ethnic terms. Such a perception along with the competitive politico-economic pressures of modernization would continue to engender an innately sectarian orientation in their thinking and behaviour. This is brought out by the three cycles in the upper part of Figure 4. The variables in the figure are measurable through scaling techniques including multi-dimensional scaling. Periodic sample surveys would serve to depict stability and change in the values of the relevant variables over the years.

(2) If the grim economic pressures of population growth, inflation, and unemployment (economic factors) during a given period intensify and persist, they would, after an experiential delay, aggravate the Perceived Grievances and Deprivation of Ethnic Group Members. The latter

would thence lead to the persistence and growth in the political alienation of the ethnic groups, and a consequential worsening of inter-communal relations (mutual distrust and tension). The periods of delay here would be empirically determinable, and may vary from a few months to a year. The speeches and writings of group leaders in the ethnic media would provide a basis for empirical verification.

Periodic sample surveys and scaling measures would bring out the nature and magnitude of time varying changes in the values of the relevant variables.

(3) If acute factionalism develops and persists in an ethnic political organization, the organization may split and alternative leaderships may emerge (Rastogi, 1975).

(4) If the population of an ethnic group is concentrated within a defined geographic area, its increasing alienation over time, would give rise to secessionist demands.

(5) If the political organization of an alienated ethnic group, covertly seeks and receives substantial monetary and other support including arms from external agencies, its sectarian orientation would become more militant. Under the influence of hostile external agencies and extremist leadership, a section of the group may actively engage in terrorism, insurgency, and subversive activities.

(6) If the ethno-political organization of a geographically concentrated group possesses large resources of arms, men and money, it would tend to engage in sustained and militant agitational political activity, including intimidation and terrorist violence to acquire power and sectarian dominance in its region. Under such conditions, intercommunal tensions would amplify over time, and lead to civil war and secession in the event of a Government's failure to cope with the situation.

(7) Random/planned acts of provocation by extremists if not checked in time by the authorities, would create disturbed law and order conditions due to an arousal of inflamed feelings in the affected community. If the disharmony between the rival communities already happens to be

high, the impact of provocative acts would precipitate large-scale disturbances and violence.

Predictive inference(s) in mode II may be similarly exemplified. This mode refers to endogenous variables deemed to be controllable by the problem-solver. The only such variable in the given system is the Government's policies. Two related variables determined by this variable are: Government's armed action, and Government's response(s). The predictive inferences and policy analysis are seen to be closely related in the present context. The nature of inferences here may be illustrated as follows:

(1)Effective and timely armed action by the Government to put down violent disturbances within a minimal period of time, would produce a cascading set of beneficial effects in the system. The individuals caught up in the disturbances would experience an early relief from violence and tension. Their life-experiences would thence record a positive image of the Government, and to that extent their ethnic self-identification would be modified by their sense of a national citizenship.

(2)Effective and timely armed action would also reduce the costs of Conflict (i.e., low loss of life and property) to opprobrious ethnic groups and the Government. Reduced cost of conflict in the system would help it recover sooner.

(3)On the other hand, if the Government's armed action is ineffective due to its inadequacy and delays, it would through its chain of impacts, lead to the persistence and growth of communal disharmony.

(4)Balanced, imaginative and unambiguous Government's response(s) to the sectarian demands of one group, and the reaction(s) of the other group, would tend to prevent an aggravation of an extant situation. If the government's response(s) are unclear, contradictory, weak and ambiguous, the resulting uncertainty and misperceptions would lead the opprobrious groups to believe that the Government can be pressurized through violent agitations and protests.

Predictive inferences in mode III are perhaps the most signigicant. Their derivation stems from the Wiener's law about the compatible and matched functioning of the constituent parts of a dynamic system (Wiener, 1958) This law in the present context signifies internally consistent and matching values of a system's salient variables[5]. At a broad level of generality, this implies the following:

(i) If the non-transient values of one or a few salient variables persist at extreme and critical levels, then the values of the remaining salient variables would also tend to become critical in a matching manner. The resultant state of the system would be very disorderly and chaotic and signify a state of civil war or break up of a society.

(ii) Similarly, if the non-transient values of some salient variables persist at a high level of viability, then the values of the remaining salient variables would also tend to become correspondingly viable, i.e., the inter-group relations would move toward harmony and cooperation.

(iii) If the values of most of the salient variables are at a given level of viability, then the non-matching viability values (high or low) of the remaining few variables, would also come (up or down) to the level of the majority of the salient variables.

The transiently high or low non-matching values of a few variables, usually, come about as a result of the sudden and powerful impact of random exogenous factors, i.e., the exogenous variables in fig. 4 and/or other national events.

The salient aspects (i.e., variables) of any given situation, would tend to display an equilibrial behavioural profile. For example, in a situation of highly opprobrious ethnic schisms, ethno-political organizations would be very strong and active, articulation of perceived grievances and deprivation would be quite high, political expression of sectional demands would be very militant, reactions of opposed groups would display high-levels of distrust and hostility, disturbed law and order conditions would recur frequently, and Government's policies would be seen as ineffective. It cannot be the case that some aspect of a situation is quite good (i.e., highly desired value of a salient variable), while the remaining ones are poor (i.e., disquietingly low values of the other salient variables). The reverse would be the case in a situation of harmonious inter-group relations.

The foregoing three modes of prediction may be seen to involve some interesting philosophical implications. While the first two modes share the concept of the cycle sequency of variables, the third mode is characterized by the concept of simultaneity in its production of predictive inferences. The philosophical implications of this duality would appear to represent a fascinating area or further research.

This chapter has outlined the trans-cultural dynamic structure of the generic problem of opprobrious relations between ethnic groups. It brings out the isomorphisms of the situations of ethnic conflict across space and time. It also provides an explanation of the phenomenon in terms of 'what','how','why' and 'when', and generates verifiable predictive inferences. The model is however, also capable of identifying the requirements of monitoring and control of ethnic conflict situations. We turn to this theme in the next chapter.

References

1. For an empirical application of the model presented here to situations in Punjab and Assam, and Hindu-Muslim tensions, see Rastogi (1986). For a detailed elaboration of the methodology of social cybernetic analysis, see Rastogi (1979, 1987, 1992).
2. Unemployment as a major causative factor in the alienation of Naga, Mizo, Manipuri and Muslim youths in India has been widely noted. The same aspect has also been noted among the Flemish in Belgium, the Catholics in Northern Ireland, and the blacks in U.K. and U.S.A Bad economic conditions have widely been noted as a major aggravating factor in the studies of ethnic conflict.
3. External agencies may provide money, arms, and training, to the disaffected elements for their own politico-military purposes.
4. The distinction between endogenous and exogenous variables is often for the analytic convenience of keeping the system's representation within limits. If a representation of the system is substantially enlarged, and its boundary expanded to include additional related aspects, then most of the exogenous variables would get incorporated as endogenous variables in the system of representation.
5. Salient variables are those which are associated with the largest number of input and output links in a multi-cycle representation. Such variables are marked with circular dots in fig. 4.

5

MONITORING AND CONTROL OF ETHNIC CONFLICT SITUATIONS

The monitoring of a problem situation is essentially concerned with following its course over time. It involves tracking the time-varying values of a limited set of variables to provide the changing picture of a situation in a synoptic manner. Monitoring is vital for a periodic appraisal of a complex problem situation. It provides the basis for initiating corrective action(s) in a timely manner to prevent a worsening of the problem. Depending upon the ap propriate periodicity of monitoring intervals, a problem-solver is enabled to receive 'early warning' or 'alert' signals about the impending changes in a problem's status. Monitoring is thus of crucial importance for detecting and identifying the changes occurring in a problem and its enviornment. It serves that vital function of minimizing the lag between situation evaluation, decision and action. In the context of the violence prone tense situations of communal conflict, a least delay appraisal of the situation can make a material difference toward saving lives and property.

IDENTIFICATION OF THE VARIABLES TO BE MONITORED

A complex situation consists of a large number of inter-acting variables. To moniter i.e., observe and measure all of them at frequent intervals may be an unmanageable task. Hence, specification of a limited set of variables to be periodically monitored is essential in this context. The variables to be selected for monitoring have to be representative of system behaviour in order to provide a valid synoptic picture of the changing states of the system. The analytic representation of the problem of ethnic tension given in the previous chapter provides a logical basis for unambiguously identifying a limited set of variables to be monitored.

In a multi-cyclical structure, certain variables may be discerned to possess a relatively large number of incoming links from, and outgoing links to, other variables. These variables stand at the intersection of several feed back cycles. They as such represent the foci of intense internal activity within a system's dynamic feed back structure. The minimum number of links associated with a variable is two i.e., one coming to it from an ante-cedent variable, and the other emanating from it to a consequent variable. A variable possessing three or more links is thence associated with two or more feed back process cycles. Larger the number of total (i.e., input and output) links surrounding variables, the more salient its status within the system. Depending on the total number of variables in a system and the requirement of a limited number of variables for monitoring, the variables possessing four or more links may be identified as the salient variables of the system. The salient variables so identified then together serve to depict the state of the system in a synoptic manner. Changes in their values over time reflect the resultant of internal system inter-actions, and external impacts, by reason of their being the foci of system's dynamics.

For the problem of inter-communal tensions, an examination of Figure 4 reveals the following set of salient variables:

1. Organization(s) for the Affirmation of Ethnic Identity and Promotion of Group Interests.
2. Perceived Grievances and Deprivation of Ethnic Group Members.
3. Political Expression of Sectarian Demands.
4. Reactions of Other Group(s).
5. Disturbed Law and Order Conditions, and
6. Government's Policies.

Each of these six variables possesses five or more links relating it to the feedback cycles and exogenous factors (figure 4). Their values at time together, represent the state of a situation of inter-communal tension at the point in time. Thus

$ET_t = [S_{1t}, S_{2t},$---------- $S_{6t}]$, and

$ET_{t'} = [S_{1t'}, S_{2t'},$--------------$S_{6t'}]$, and so on.

where ET is the state of a situation of ethnic tension, S_1, S_2,-------S_6 are its salient variables as above, and *t* and *t'* are two successive time periods. The concept of salient variables in a multi-cyclical structure thus enables one to identify a limited set of variables for monitoring a complex problem situation.

MEASUREMENT OF MONITORED VARIABLES

The six salient variables identified for monitoring need to be measured at periodic intervals in order to provide successive appraisals of a problem situation over time.

The salient variable, organization(s) for the Affirmation of Ethnic Identity and Promotion of Group Interests, may be measured by the proportion of ethnic population displaying high empathy and/or affiliation with the exclusivist ethnic organization(s)[1] This formulation incorporates the essence of the variable for the purposes of a synoptic appraisal through its monitoring. Other cognate aspects of this variable i.e., the number of organizations, the nature of their activities, their total membership, their history, media, and leadership, etc; are relevant for inclusion in a management information system for the problem concerned. But for the purposes of periodic synoptic appraisals, the proportion of motivated and empathic population affiliated to the sectarian organization(s) is a suitable and adequate indicator. Alternatively, a schema of composite measurement based on multi-dimensional scaling and including several indicators may be formulated.

The salient variable, Perceived Grievances and deprivation of Ethnic Group Members, may be measured similarly by the proportion of mobilized and activist ethnic population believing itself, and/or its group, as deprived/discriminated/disadvantaged in relation to other communal groups. The variable, Political Expression of Sectarian Demands is measured qualitatively in terms of increasingly extreme stances of sectarian political demands. The scale values of 1 and 0 here would correspond to a 'complete absence of sectarian demands and protests' and 'demand for complete independence through unlimited violence' respectively.

The scale value of 0.25 would denote a 'low level of orderly political activity around modest demands', a value of 0.5 would correspond to 'demands for differential previleges/benefits and serious allegations of discrimination and neglect', and a value of 0.75 would stand for 'secessionist demands for independent political identity'. The scale values of demands coming under the scope of any value zone would be estimated within the range of values in that zone. The variable, reaction of other groups, may analogously be measured as the proportion of population of other ethnic group(s) strongly opposed to the disaffected group's demands.

The Variable,, Disturbed Law and Order Conditions, is measurable qualitatively in terms of an increasing level of violence against persons and property. The scale values of 0 and 1 here would correspond to a 'complete absence of disruptive communal disharmony' and a 'full scale civil war' respectively. The scale value of 0.25 may stand for 'minor and rare situations of communal disharmony' 0.5 may denote 'organized agitations and disorders and infrequent violent disturbances', and 0.75 may correspond to 'recurrent and extensive violent riots, growing phases of guerilla war,terrorism and insurgency, substantial loss of life and property with disruptive effect on the economy'. The intermediate types of situations would be assessable in terms of their placement within appropriate scaling zones. The remaining salient variable, Government policies, is also measurable in terms of an effectiveness scale from 0 to 1 . The assignment of performance values to variables would depend on substantial empirical evidence, insight into the nature of a given situation, and accumulated experience in the context of that situation.

MONITORING AND CONTROL OF THE POTENTIAL FOR VIOLENCE

A more important issue in the present context is an appraisal of the potentiality for inter-ethnic violence. If such a potentiality could be assessed at an early stage before the phase of violence begins, an early and timely implementation of relevant control measures may prove to be more effective in reducing the problem's magnitude and severity. This problem- solving insight however, poses the issues of detecting and deciding what to monitor.

Potential for recourse to violence including terrorism by an ethnic group, or its section(s), may be identified from one or more of the following system variables. Political Expression of Sectarian Demands may involve oral and written utterances of communal leaders regarding their proclivities for recourse to violence. Reactions of other group(s), may also similarly permit one to discern the group's propensity for violence for protecting and advancing its interests. Manifestations of Mutual Distrust and Tension, through the speeches and writings of the leaders from antagonistic groups, may also disclose recurring references to the possibilities for violence. If the tendency toward violence is referred to as a *k* factor, and is seen to be recurrently present in one or more of the foregoing three variables, a distinct potential for violence may be deemed to exist.

Reinforcement of a potential for violence i.e., the *k* factor requires another complementary factor *K'*. Factor *K'* refers to one or both the groups' acquisition of arms, their storage, and training in their use. Sources of acquisition may be overt and/or covert. Factors *K* and *K'* are mutually reinforcing as follows:

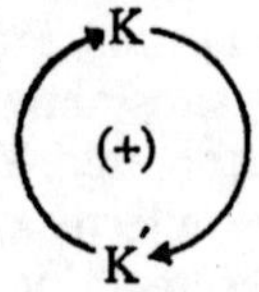

Fig. 5: Mutual re-inforcement of factors promoting violence

This simple positive feed back cycle means that the stronger a group's tendency toward a recourse to violence (i.e., *K*), the greater would be its attempts to acquire arms for 'preparing' to defend its 'just interests' (*K'*). The more and better the armed preparation, of group, the greater would be its tendency toward their use i.e., recourse to violence. If the mutually reinforcing factors *K* and *K'* are present together in a non-transient manner, they would engender disturbed law and order conditions. The latter may range from sporadic violent clashes to terrorism, riots, insurgency, rebellion, and civil war.

Detecting and monitoring the factors *K* and *K'* are important. If they can be brought under control at an early stage, a situation's potential for violence may be surgically removed. Its evolution and amplification toward turbulent violence would thence be halted for the immediate future. This short term control measure may thus provide the national problem-solvers more time for proceeding toward a steady-state long term solution of the problem.

Identification of the factors *K* and *K'*, their utility in anticipating a situation's progression toward violence, and thence proceeding toward their nullification, represent a meaningful example of the problems' isomorphism at the level of their short term control. Such control inferences would be valid for every serious situation of ethno-social conflict with appropriate contextual variations.

SHORT TERM POLICY MEASURES FOR THE CONTROL OF CONFLICT SITUATIONS

Policy measures for controlling situations of ethnic conflict, stem from the requirements of regulating and improving the values of the problem's salient variables. These policy measures comprise the requirements of problem solution both in the short and long term perspectives. The long term measures are also intrinsically related to the issues of national integration. They are elucidated in the next two chapters. Here we focus on the short term policy measures. Apart from the foregoing important requirement of monitoring and control of a situation's potential for violence, other policy measures may briefly be outlined as follows:

(i) Effective and timely armed action, by a Government to control disturbed law and order conditions, within a minimal period of time would produce beneficial effects on the situation. Persons caught up in the disturbances would experience an early relief from tension and violence. Their life-experiences, would thence record a positive image of the government, and to that extent their ethnic self-identification may be modified by a sense of national citizenship.

(ii) Effective and timely action would also reduce the costs of conflict (i.e., loss of life and property), to the nation and communities.

(iii) If the Government's control of a situation is ineffective owing to inadequacy and delays, it would through its chain of impacts, lead to persistence and growth of ethnic disharmony and distrust. It would also adversely affect the Government's image, and problem-solving capability.

(iv) Balanced, imaginative, and unambiguous, Government's responses to sectarian demands of one group, and to reactions of other group(s), would tend to prevent an aggravation of a prevailing situation. If the Government's responses are unclear, contradictory, weak, and ambiguous, the resultant perceptions and misconceptions, would lead the opprobrious groups to believe that their sectional objectives may best be achieved through militancy and violence.

(v) Flow of funds and arms from abroad, must be checked in a decisive manner, through interdiction of such supplies and diplomatic efforts.

(vi) Occurrence of random/planned provocative acts, must be checked through use of intelligence machinery.

(vii) Dissensions and divisions within militant ethno-political organizations, may be promoted to control the hate and conflict potential of the organized political expression of their sectarian demands i.e., agitations.

(viii) Government must not only eliminate all forms of overt and covert discrimination based on ethnicity, but should also be seen to do so. This would tend to weaken an ethnic group's perceived grievances and deprivation.

(ix) Sectarian political activities of ethno-political organizations should be effectively curbed. Spread of hate propaganda, and ideology of ethnic chauvinism through public platforms, religious places, and ethnic media, must be prevented.

The foregoing policy measures for the problem's solution need to be implemented conjointly and effectively. In so far as, however, terrorist violence is a very grim and dark part of an acute problem situation, its control would need a set of strong operational measures which are outlined next.

OPERATIONAL MEASURES FOR CONTROLLING TERRORIST VIOLENCE

The nature of operational measures needed for reducing and controlling the depredations of terrorists in the form of wanton killings, murders, and massacres, of innocent men, women, and children, may briefly be indicated as follows:

I. Vigilance concerning and the monitoring of the movements of terrorists, arms smugglers, and drug traffickers, and their interdiction.

II. Increasing the strength of security forces. This measure is related to the field ratio of security personnel per terrorist or insurgent. Empirical researches into the nature of guerrilla wars and insurgency in various parts of the world have estimated the requirements of this ratio at 8 (Deitchman, 1962; Braun *et al*, 1983).

III. Detection and capture of offenders and their collaborators through intelligence work.

IV. Improved collection of intelligence through sophisticated devices.

V. Vigilance against the inflow of foreign and domestic funds to subversive organizations and individuals.

VI. Freedom of operations to security forces for the capture of terrorists and their stock of arms.

VII. Effective training and indoctrination of security personnel in anti-terrorist operations.

VIII. Improved equipment and logistics of security forces.

IX. Detection and removal of terrorist infiltrators/sympathisers from the ranks of local police and administration.

X. Search and destroy operations against suspected hideouts/bases.

XI. Rehabilitation of terrorists willing to surrender.

XII. Arming of sections vulnerable to terrorists' attacks.

XIII. Locating and disrupting terrorists' channels and stocks of arms supply.

XIV. Ensuring secrecy of security operations.

XV. Eliminating delays and coordination weaknesses in the chain of information-decision-action at local, regional and national levels.

XVI. Stoppage of political interference in security operations.

XVII. Incentives to, and persuasion of, local people toward help in anti-terrorist operations.

XVIII. Seizing the initiative from the terrorists gangs by raising their cost of conflict.

Foregoing operational measures are not easy to implement, but they are vital for the control of terrorist violence. In the absence of their effective execution, not only would an acute problem situation remain uncontrollable, but the long term policy measures for a steady-state solution of opprobrious ethnic relations, also cannot be properly implemented. The skills, resources, and motivation of terrorists and insurgents need to be more than matched by the Government's security apparatus, in this context.

Long term policy/solution measures on the other hand, would require a conjoint and coordinated set of programmes involving compulsory education of the young in universal human values, creative use of mass media for the propagation of humanistic and spiritual ideals, control of population growth and generation of economic opportunities based on sustained economic growth (Rastogi, 1986). The nature and dimensions of a long term or steady-state solution of the problem, are explicated in the next two chapters.

References

1. The reference to ethnic population here is to be considered at the spatial level of the problem's analysis i.e., local, or regional, or national, as may be the case. Sophisticated use of sampling techniques would be necessary in the context of measurements here.

6

ISSUES IN NATIONAL INTEGRATION AND POLICY REQUIREMENTS

The problem of national integration is not a political problem. The serious implications of its non-resolution i.e., the prevalence of opprobrious ethnic schisms in a pluralistic society may, however, have serious political implications for the stability and growth of a nation. National integration is largely a psychological problem, i.e., one involving the perceptions and world views of the members of various ethnic groups. If the members of ethnic collectivities perceive and identify themselves as parts of a larger harmonious whole, then the problem's very basis would not exist. If on the other hand, one or more of such groups give primacy to the perceived interests of their own group, regardless of the interests of other sections, and are prone to use violent means for the pursuit of their exclusive sectional goals, then situation or ethnic conflict emerge, and weaken the centripetal forces integrating the polity of a nation. The 'what','why','how', and 'when', of such situations were elucidated in chapter four. The goals of national integrations, or rather the goal-state of the solution of this problem, may then be seen to be operationally definable in terms of the solution of the problem of ethnic tensions and conflict.

THE GOAL STATE OF NATIONAL INTEGRATION

The goal state of the national integration problem may thence be delineated by the following characterization or status of the salient variables of the dynamic structure of ethnic conflicts:

(i) Transition of ethnic organizations from active politico-cultural collectivities, to purely cultural entities, interacting with other similar entities in harmonious exchange relationships of mutual enrichment.

(ii) Replacement of ethnic grievances, with common grievances of nation's citizens, towards a better quality of life for all.

(iii) Substitution of political expression of sectarian demands, by political participation toward non-sectarian demands, for welfare of all citizens.

(iv) Transformation of the distrustful and opprobrious reaction of other group(s) toward shared perceptions and concerns.

(v) Null values of disturbed law and order conditions engendered by ethnic conflict.

(vi) Effectiveness of Government's policies, toward promotion of social harmony, and national self-identification, of citizens.

Realization of the goal-state of problem-solution (defined by the desired status of the problem's salient variables), calls for a conjunctive and sustained application, of both short and long term policy measures. The short term policy measures were outlined in chapter five. Long term measures are discussed next. These measures highlight and address the basic issues involved in achieving the above goals of national integration.

BASIC ISSUES AND LONG TERM POLICY MEASURES

The basic issues involved in achieving the goal-state of national integration may be elaborated briefly as follows. They are identifiable from the generic dynamic structure of the problem in Fig. 4

I. The most basic issue of national integration is highlighted by the very first variable of Fig4. Perceived Ethnic Basis of Self-Identity by Individuals, and the primacy accorded to it by group members over a larger national identity, is a major issue impeding the efforts toward national integration. It sets the stage for the divisive ethno-politics of groups based on their parochial interests and goals.

II. The second major issue, related to the first is the Sectarian Socio-Political Orientation of the members of ethnic groups. Ethnic consciousness does not remain confined to cultural traditions, sentiments, and interests. It graduates toward communal chauvinism, which in turn, becomes a dominant factor in the group members' antagonistic pursuit of their narrow politico-economic interests/objectives.

III. The third issue is the Perceived Grievances and Deprivation of Ethnic Group Members. Proclivity toward perception and definition of problems and difficulties faced by the people in terms of their being members of a particular socio-cultural group, serves to fragment the national polity, and weakens the bases of national integration.

IV. The fourth impeding issue related to the third is the Political Expression of Sectarian Demands of militant ethno-political organizations. Competition for leadership within these organizations aggravates the situation of social divisiveness and tensions at the national level. In so far as, the very basis of an ethno-political organization, is the exclusivist promotion of the interests of its own ethnic group, the competition for leadership in such an organization leads to a continuing invention and escalation of sectarian demands by its leaders in their bid to mobilize support for themselves. Such a process fosters ethnic schisms and antagonisms, and generates opprobrious reactions/responses from other groups.

V. The fifth major impeding issue related to fourth is the Reaction(s) of Other Group(s). They tend to impart a momentum to the processes of social divisiveness and disharmony.

VI. Mutual Distrust and Tensions between groups generated by the pathological interaction of (IV) and (V), become the most visible and dominant issue impeding the process of national reconciliation and unity. Their continuing growth and persistence leads to induction of violence in inter-group relationships.

VII. Recurrent riots, destructive activities, terrorism, rebellion, insurgency, and civil war may variously follow in the wake of the induction of violence in inter-group relations. Factors *K* and *K'* described in chapter five, come into play in this phase. This phase signifies the process of national disintegration, whose eventual outcome may be the break-up of a national society system.

VIII. Another important issue in the present context is related to the Government policies. If they are oriented toward the politics of 'vote banks', toward appeasement of communal groups for political gain, and toward fostering inter-group cleavages for electoral/political benefits, the process of national integration would not only be weakened, but it would also lose credibility. The resultant anomie and alienation in political interdiction, would severely undermine the moral foundations of the state, its agents/agencies, and their actions.

The foregoing impeding issues or blocking factors of national integration, can be addressed and rectified only in terms of a sustained implementation of long term policy measures. Before however, considering the nature and dimensions of such measures, the flaws and deficiencies of existing national policies, need to be understood in the present context.

FLAWED NATIONAL POLICIES

While all the national political leaders and the Government unanimously stress their commitment toward national unity and integration, their policies and actions contradict their professed objective. The following aspects of the country's political processes, and Government policies, bring out this contradiction, clearly:

I. All the national political parties focus on the caste arithmetic in electoral constituencies while setting up their candidates for elections to state and central legislatures. Such a political practice reinforces the caste and communal identities for various social groups.

II. Communal political parties are allowed to function freely, and engage in their propaganda of ethnic separatism. Some of the national parties also enter into electoral alliances with them. These practices directly promote the politics of ethnic divisiveness and foster the development of communalism in national polity.

III. All political parties try to build up their 'vote banks' based on the considerations of caste, community,language, religion, and region. For this purpose, they often try to promote distinctly sectional interests and demands. Such practices lead to fragmentation of national polity on the one hand, and blockage of the emergence of a commonly shared sense of national identity, on the other.

IV. Both State and Central Governments often set up official and semi-official organs meant for the benefits of specific sections of people such as 'backward' castes, scheduled castes, and Muslims. Instead of viewing and caring for the economic interests and social welfare of people irrespective of their social origin, these tactics are resorted to for narrow political gains. They, in turn, serve to reinforce narrow group consciousness among the people on the one hand, and their political mobilization on the basis of socially divisive forces, on the other.

V. Casteist and communal pressure groups and organizations are actively though covertly cultivated by the political parties and leaders. This lends them respectability on the one hand, and increases their potential for social divisiveness, on the other.

VI. The attempts by various political parties to capitalize on the issue of caste-based reservations in government jobs both at the state and central levels contribute directly toward heightening the caste consciousness of people, and in directly toward strengthening the politics of caste and community. Their failure to evolve and develop a reservation policy as an instrument of social justice for the poor irrespective of their caste and communal affiliations, attests to the existence of a wide gap between their theory and practice in the context of national integration.

There exists, thus, a marked disparity between the professed policies, and the actual practices, of both the political parties and the government of the country. Such a gap has served to reduce the credibility of official efforts to promote national integration. They are not taken seriously by the people who are encouraged to think of themselves more as the members of particular groups, than as the citizens of a cohesive nation. Such a gap also raises serious questions about the capability of existing national institutions, and apparatus of governance, to implement the difficult long term policy measures required for achieving the objectives of national integration.

LONG TERM POLICY MEASURES

The nature and dimensions of long term policy measures for a steady-state solution of the problem(s) of internal social schism or national integration, also stem from the generic structure of the situation as depicted in Fig. 4 They may very briefly be outlined as follows:

[I] Socialization and education of the young generation need to be restructured toward instilling in them the universal moral humanistic values. The universalistic values have to be accorded primacy in the minds of the future citizens over the sectarian and narrow self-images and world-views of the members of their communities. Such a restructuring would imply that the consciousness of ethnic identity remains confined to the cultural sentiments and concerns only, and does not lead to an internalization of ethnic chauvinism or exclusivism. The thrust of problem-solving endeavour here is toward weakening the Perceived Ethnic Basis of Self-Identity by Individuals, and promoting the universalistic ideals of goodwill, harmony, tolerance, kindness, service, and charity toward all human beings irrespective of their social or ethnic labels.

[II] Political Expression of Sectarian Demand needs to be checked, devalued, and replaced by healthy and orderly political processes oriented toward serving the needs and aspirations of all people as a single collectivity. Ethno-politics of parochial group interests needs to be eliminated. Propaganda channels based on the socially divisive ideologies of hate, chauvinism, and sectarianism need to be closed. Communal political parties should be rendered inoperative as part of a systematic and sustained efforts to re-design the country's political system and processes. The participation of sectarian organizations in the nation's political system, needs to be abolished. The thrust of efforts here is toward rendering Organization(s) for the Affirmation of Ethnic Identity and Promotion of Group Interests, non-functional.

[III] Mass media of communication in all forms should be mobilized effectively toward the sustained propagation of universalistic moral human values on the one hand, and the discrediting of narrow, sectarian ethno-politics on the other. This would call for a redirection of the media policy, and a redefinition of its functions. All the channels and media of mass communication should be reoriented toward changing the socially divisive communal perceptions and world-views of the people as a whole. The thrust of efforts here is toward eliminating the Sectarian Socio-Political Orientation of Group Members, besides the spread of social virtues, goodwill, and harmony among the people at large.

A crucially important role of mass media in the present context would be to remove the dark subjective images, fears, and apprehensions, in the minds of the members of opprobrious communities toward each other. Such dark fears and apprehensions need to be convincingly refuted by exposing them to the light of calm understanding, proper knowledge, and informed reflective reasoning, on the mass public plane. This role is very necessary and important for removing the psychic miasma of distrust and suspicion between groups. Removal of distrust is vitally necessary for providing support to the efforts toward national unity.

[IV] The Government's treatment of all citizens of the country must be manifestly non-partisan. Differences of religion, caste, region, and language, should be strictly regarded as irrelevant in respecting the rights of citizens, and/or in the measures meant for their welfare. All the organs of the Government must deal with the citizens in a demonstrably fair, efficient, courteous, and uniform manner. All the facilities, opportunities, and services, provided by the Government must be available to them on an egalitarian and non-discriminatory basis. The thrust of efforts here is toward overcoming the Perceived Grievance and Deprivation of Ethnic Group Members, and rendering the Organizations for the Promotion of Group Interests, non-functional.

[V] A crucially important and obvious measure is to promote and strengthen the process of economic development efficiently and effectively. This measure aims at reducing the severe pressures of inflation and unemployment, so that they do not aggravate an ethnic group's perceived sense of grievances and deprivation. Moral and humanistic values may be difficult to sustain amidst serious economic problems faced by a nation's population. Economic developmental efforts should be supplemented by the efforts to regulate the growth of population, and remove illiteracy of the masses. Illiteracy removal programme should also become a part of a developmental communication strategy toward fostering the moral, spiritual and humanistic values amongst the masses. In the absence of economic opportunities, however,the receptivity of the masses toward, the emission of planned and positive communicative stimuli, would be low.

[VI] The Government's responses, as well as, those of the political parties need to be focused on nation-building as distinct from their tendency hitherto, toward deriving short term political advantages from events and situations in the country. The Government's response has also to be clear, consistent, and unambiguous in the face of severe political pressures from powerful groups. Ambiguous and dilatory responses may often worsen a bad situation, and send erroneous signals regarding the firmness of the Government's resolve and position.

[VII] Cultural expression of the group's identity must be made consistant with the requirements of their integration at the national level. Otherwise the disruptive potential of ethnic exclusivism and chauvinism may damage a humane political system based on the values of tolerance and liberty.

[VIII] The programme of mass communication and the implementation of short and long term policy measures must support, sustain, and reinforce one another. The measures like prevention of riots and terrorism; abolition of sectarian politics; curbing of media and channels of communal hatred and chauvinism, and their realignment toward ethnic harmony; impartial treatment of all citizens by the Government; economic development; and regulation of cultural expression of ethnicity with a non-sectarian political frame, need to be complemented by effective communication measures. In the absence of the latter, the impact of control measures may be weak, and non-cumulative. Reciprocally, in the absence of credible control measures, the communication efforts would be rendered ineffective owing to a 'credibility gap'

CONTROL AND PROBLEM-SOLVING

Both short and long term policy/solution measures are needed to reduce and resolve the problems of ethnic strife and national integration. Short term measures are concerned with the control of problem's disruptive symptoms, while long term measures are oriented toward realizing a vision of inter-group peace, harmony, and cooperation. Both the sets of measures are essentially complementary, and can often be implemented in a parallel and conjunctive manner. But long term measures would appear to be properly applicable in a situation only when the short term measures are effectively operative in that situation.

The fundamental guidance for control and problem solving is provided by the Ashby's Law of Requisite Variety (Ashby 1956; Rastogi, 1979). According to this law, the necessary condition of control is that the problem solver must have at his disposal at least as many appropriate regulatory responses as are the aspects and forms of the problem situation to be controlled. In the absence of adequate matching number of appropriate responses, the control or full regulation would not be possible in principle. The sufficient condition is that out of the responses available to the system controller, at least one or more must be effective against the dimensions of the situation encountered from time to time. A complementary sufficient condition is the timeliness of response implementaion. A problem solving response must not only match the problem's nature and be effective against it, but must also be timely. A tardy and delayed response would seriously depreciate the efficacy of response implementation.

The role of analysis, explanation, predictive inferences, monitoring, evaluation, and identification of policy measures, is to enable the societal problem-solver(s) to resolve the difficult issues of national integration on the basis of knowledge, values and reasoning. Much more, however,is needed in this context in the form of motivation and commitment, values and vision on the part of the problem-solver(s).

7

ETHNIC SCHISMS AND NATIONAL INTEGRATION

Ethno-social conflict refers to oppugnancy between human groups differing in their perceptions of their respective ethnic identities. This conflict is a grim facet of man's social history across space and time. In its acute form, it produces within a society, death and destruction, suffering and agony, hate and rage, bitterness and sorrow, grieving parents and benumbed orphans, and physically and psychologically mutilated wrecks and destitutes. In this sense, ethno-social conflict is an important part of the wider problem of human misery. This chapter attempts to analyse the nature of this pervasive larger problem. Psycho-social factors underlying its production in social systems are sought to be identified. They may lead us toward a more basic steady-state solution of the given problem. Due to its pervasive nature, the problem of human misery is bound up with the basics of individual psychology and social inter action.

HUMAN MISERY IN SOCIAL SYSTEMS

Human beings live in social systems. Social systems comprise patterned human inter actions. Misery and suffering refer to unpleasant, contra-survival experiences of man in social systems. These experiences are generated by persons interacting as subjects and/or objects. Human misery is thus produced in and through human inter action itself. Mental diseases and suicide in this context represent, self-induced states of human misery. These states may, however, be cumulative outcomes over time of the inter actions of the persons concerned.

Human misery is ubiquitous. Man's capacity to inflict suffering on fellowman is awsome. Cruelty, deceit, greed, humiliation, revenge, murder, rape, dacoity, sadism, violence, wanton destruction of property, implication of innocents in criminal cases, injustice, turning rural poor into bonded labourers or serfs through deceit and usury, kidnapping for sexual assault or ransom, harassment of citizens by corrupt officials, use of terror and torture for political and criminal ends, forced prostitution, mutilation of children for beggary, dowry deaths, bribery, nepotism, brazen indiscipline, wilful negligence of duties, coercion, brutalities against children and prisoners, drug addiction and peddling, embezzlement, misappropriation of funds for the poor, blackmarketing, adulteration of food stuffs and commodities, bogus medicines, ethnic antagonisms and chauvanism, large scale religious/racial/communal violence, brutal internal civil wars, 'limited' wars, and those involving chemical, bacteriological and nuclear weapons of mass destruction, are sample of man's capacity as a profuse producer of misery.[1]

The resultant states of the social systems are variously depicted by disintegrating and broken families; rudderless juvenile delinquents; warped children and adolescents; hapless victims of murder, rape, and crime, searching pathetically for justice; orphaned and starving children; destitute widows and old men; burned brides; hardworking and honest persons reduced to penury by mob violence; catatonic alcoholic and drug addicts; increasing cases of mental stress, depression, diseases, 'madness' and suicide; thousands working as slaves i.e., bonded labourers in the rural areas; enriched criminals, corrupt officials and unscrupulous businessmen dominating social life; flourishing criminal syndicates, racketeers and black-mailers; politicians with criminal links; communal/religious/racial chauvinists and bigots terrorising and killing helpless persons; refugees fleeing from death and dishonour; mounting expenditures on police and military while millions continue to suffer from squalor, illiteracy, disease, and malnutrition; and a general social milieu of decay, cynicism, hopelessness, and despair. The phenomenon of human agony and misery is widespread across men and nations of the globe.

THE MISERY-PRODUCING ACT (MpA) AND SOCIAL CONTROL

A voluntary act by a person resulting in misery for others is often explicitly recognized as criminal and reprehensible. The perpetrator of such an act is thence derogatively labelled. A social order employs control mechanisms of social censure and legal punishment to curb such acts. A premeditated murder for example is recognized as a reprehensible act. It elicits deterrent punishment of life-imprisonment/death. The perpetrator of this act is designated as a 'murderer' and viewed with acute revulsion. Other misery-producing reprehensible acts like rape, sadism, dacoity, bride burning, criminal harassment, food poisoning, etc; and their executors are also analogously labelled and condemned for severe punishment.

An unfortunate fact, however, is that despite provision of deterrent punishments and severe social censure, graphs of misery-producing acts (MpAs) and indicators of suffering do not show downward trend. Persistence and growth of MpAs thence bring out inadequacies and failures of social control mechanisms. Weaknesses of the latter may also arise from following factors:

(i) The law and order enforcement personnel may be incompetent and/or unmotivated.

(ii) In many situations involving blackmail and/or terror, victims may not even be in position to reveal their misery i.e., such acts may go unrecorded.

(iii) A Government itself may sanction oppressive measures, violence and torture against a section or group of persons on the grounds of their actual or suspected opposition to the ruling regime.[2]

(iv) Large scale violence and complex issues between antagonistic ethnic groups may not be amenable to solution within the limited perspective of law and order problems.

Due to above reasons, the efficacy or social control mechanisms for removing misery (or MpAs) appears limited. Their limitation is further highlighted when we consider complementary problem of self-induced states of misery (SIM_s).

SELF-INDUCED STATE OF HUMAN MISERY (SIM_p)

A man may experience misery as a result of intended and/or unintended act(s) of other person(s) towards him. He may, however, also experience misery as a result of his own psychological and psycho-physical disturbances. These disturbances may be cumulative outcomes of a series of anxiety-laden actions and events. Unhappy inter-personal relationships, disrupted social bonds, thwarted ambitions, and frustrated efforts, may produce continuing mental stress in an individual resulting in mental diseases. Acute anxiety and tension, neurosis, psychosis, compulsive reaction patterns, schizophrenia, catatonia, manic-depressive psychosis, morbidity, madness, and suicide, etc; represent various forms and modes of self-engendered states of human misery.

Diseases like hypertension, heart condition, blood pressure, proneness to cancer, angina pectoris, and emphysema, are also known to have their roots in chronic problems of psychological stress and maladjustment. More and more diseases are being adjudged to have psycho-social origins. As a matter of fact, public health authorities in western countries are coming to another novel conclusion in this context. According to them, biggest scope for improving public health may lie in measures that change in social behaviour, rather than increasing the supply of medical care.

TWO DIMENSIONS OF MISERY

Problem of human misery may thus be seen to have two dimensions — external and internal. External dimension refers to infliction of misery as a consequence of a voluntary human act. Internal dimension refers to an inner state of misery induced by psychological and/or psycho-physical disturbances. These disturbances may however, have been brought about by frustrating experiences of an individual in his social relationships, and/or goal seeking endeavours. Mechanisms of social control are seen to be flawed in their application to external dimension of human misery. For internal dimension, they are inapplicable. Hence, the problem of overcoming human misery needs an inclusive approach that may deal both with MPAs and misery producing internal emotional turmoils (SIMs). Such an approach would, however, need to examine cognitive and affective bases of human action.

COGNITIVE AND AFFECTIVE BASES OF HUMAN ACTION

A voluntary act by a human being is invariably associated with its concomitant cognitive and affective bases. They account for decision(s) leading to that act. Affective base refers to configuration of motives, emotions, and drives, that arouses and/or precipitates an action. Cognitive base refers to a person's frame(s) of reference and definition(s) of situation(s). It comprises a person's means-ends schema and internalized code(s) of choice. Frames of reference and situations definitions are cumulative results of one's experiences and perceived interests. During any action situation, conation i.e., the act is matched and backed up by its accompanying cognition and affect counter-parts. Behaviour of a person is characterized by its coherence and psychic organization.

Cognition, affect, and conation, tend to be mutually consistent with one another. The consistency characteristic may be represented as follows:

COGNITION = AFFECT = CONATION

This cosistency relationship implies that there are no contradictions or incompatibilities between themes of cognition, emotive drives, and act. In case of serious contradictions, man's capacity to act tends to be paralysed. Consistency relationship is however, not static or rigid. All three aspects of a human action situation may concomitantly be modified over time in terms of their dynamic feedback inter-relationships. Modification and changes may be results of past actions and changing environmental conditions. Appraisal of results may produce changes in a person's cognitive frame and emotive configuration in terms of his learning and experience.

COGNITIVE AND AFFECT SUPPORT SYSTEMS OF MpAs AND SIMs

Requirement of consistency amongst affect, cognition, and conation, elements serves to elucidate psychic support systems of misery producing act (MpAs). Basic issue here is:

Given a MpA (e.g., murder, rape), what is (are) motivational/emotional drive(s) that led to the act's consideration and execution? And what cognitive frame of reference enabled the offending actor to justify/rationalize his criminal act in conformity with his motivational/emotional drive(s)?

Analysis of this issue may then possibly enable one to come across promising insights into problems of misery and conflict.

Affect and cognitive support systems of MpAs may be identified through empirical case studies of such acts. Analysis of murder cases and murderers may for example, reveal a set of recurrent and varying combinations of motives/emotions of revenge, greed, anger, bitterness, fear, and hatred, underlying a MpA of murder. Similarly, acts of rape may almost invariably be associated with motivational drive of lust, although in some cases desire to humiliate victims may also be present. In cases of violent dacoity, dominant motives may be those of greed and cruelty. In cases of corruption and bribery, motivational drive of greed may be supplemented by desire for luxuries and/or social prestige through amassed wealth. In cases of poors' exploitation, motivations may be those of greed, selfishness, and contempt.

In self-induced states of misery (SIM$_s$) like severe mental depression, 'madness' and suicide, dominating emotions and feelings may be of utter helplessness, acute frustration with life, emotional turmoil, enveloping despair, and overpowering hopelessness. There may also be situations where despair and frustrations lead to aggressive acts classifiable as MpAs. In such situation, an individual in a state of misery (SIM$_s$) may inflict misery on other (MpA). All these varied examples bring out crucial and preponderant role of limited sets of abnormal and disturbed emotions/motives (e*/m*s) that impel an individual toward specific MpAs or SIM$_s$.

The reasoning here shows that misery-producing reprehensible acts like murder, rape, and violent dacoity, as well as, internal conditions of mental illness and suicide, etc.; are impelled by and psychically consistent with a given set of abnormal emotional/motivational states. Such a representation and analysis then point toward a solution approach for the misery problem as follows:

Find one or more *affect operators* that may diminish and/or nullify (e*/m*s) contained in an emotive set producing a MpA or SIM$_s$. If (e*/m*s) for a particular MpA or SIM$_s$ are weakened and/or nullified by such *affect operators*, then that particular MpA and/or SIM$_s$ would not be precipitated.

Assuming that one or more such nullifying operators are identified, then the requirement of consistency would call forth a reconstructed cognitive frame of reference for an individual. Identification of nullifying affect operators and cognitive frame of reference consistent with them, would be discussed later. We now turn to analyse cognitive framework of MpAs.

COGNITIVE FRAME OF REFERENCE OF MpAs

In terms of foregoing discussion, the issue here may be posed as follow:

Given a MpA (e.g., murder, rape) and a concomitant set of abnormal and disturbed emotions and motives $<e_1^*/m_1$, e_2^*/m_2^*.......... $>$ what cognitive frame of reference enables the offending individual to justify/rationalize his MpA ?

An individual's cognitive frame of reference comprises his subjective means-end schema, and code(s) of choice regarding human relationships, institutional norms, and self-interests. Cognitive base of a MpA can be identified by uncovering implicit and explicit assumptions of offending individuals behind their voluntary execution of that MpA. Consider for example a case of a pre-planned murder and a case of rape. Both of these voluntary actions reveal certain common presumptions of offending actors. For example, in both instances one finds as follows.

(C1) Victim i.e., a fellow human being is perceived and treated as an object to be manipulated and used (i.e., deprived of life in one case, and of respect and dignity in the other)[3].

(C2) Victims moral rights as a person, and civic rights as a citizen, are deemed to be non-existent or irrelevant in the context of offending actor's motives and interests (i.e., greed and hatred in one case, and lust in the other). Thus the very recognition of an universal moral code governing human relationships is denied.

(C3) Wilful nature of the two MpAs also shows their executors contemptuous disregard of their society's law and order machinery.

(C4) Murder and rape (MpAs) are accepted and resorted to by actors as necessary means for their perceived ends including emotive gratification.

Same presumption is seen to be operative in other MpAs as well. Suppose we next consider a case of dacoity and case of bribery. Here too, in both instances one may find as follows:

(C1) Victim is perceived and treated by offending actors as an object, or thing, to be made use of (i.e., deprived of money by force and violence in one case, and of benefit(s) due to victim, in the other).

(C2) Victim's moral and civic rights are viewed as irrelevant by actors in the context of their craving for unearned wealth.

(C3) Recourse to dacoity and bribery by actors as an accepted practice on their part, shows their contemptuous evalution of their society's police and legal system.

(C4) Dacoity and bribery (MpAs) are accepted and resorted to by actors as necessary means for gratifying their lust for wealth.

Similar cognitive elements operative in the mental world-view of a violent communalist may be outlined as follows:

(C1) Victims i.e., fellow human beings belonging to an opposed ethnic community, are perceived and treated as personifications of the hateful and vicious communal enemy, who have no right to 'life'.

(C2) Victims' moral and civic rights are deemed irrelevant in the context of the offending actor's motives and interests (i.e., hate, rage, and bitterness toward the 'enemy' group that wants to destroy 'us').

(C3) Recourse to rioting involving violence, arson, and killings by the actor (i.e., communalist rioter) shows his contemptuous disregard of the society's law and order machinery.

(C4) Violence, arson, and killing, are accepted and resorted to by the actor as necessary means for the preservation of his community's 'honour', and interests, and for gratifying his lust for revenge.

Same paradigm with minor contextual variations is seen to emerge out of other MpAs like exploitation of poor, prostitution, drug peddling, dowry deaths, and so on. With appropriate contextual modifications, this paradigm may also be applied to self-induced states of misery (SIMs) like mental depression, diseases, 'madness' and suicide. Here, an individual comes to perceive himself as a helpless object manipulated by, and/or at mercy of other persons and forces. He himself becomes, oblivious of his moral status, civic duties, legal right, and social obligations. With increasing loss of will power and self-confidence, his cognitive framework tends to become a passive mirror image that of an aggressive perpetrator of MPAs. In the cognitive frame of SIM$_s$, the signs of themes in a MPA frame may be viewed as reversed.

Four broad themes of the above paradigm may be seen as defining a general cognitive frame of reference (i.e., the mental make-up) of the perpetrators of MPAs. The problematic misery may also be represented as follows:

$\langle C1, C2, C3, C4 \rangle = MPAs$

This expression shows that a cognitive set consisting of premises C1 to C4 is consistent with the voluntary execution of MPAs. Since the principle of consistency operates over cognition, conation, and affect dimensions in a conjoint manner, this cognitive frame of reference would be consistent with the configuration of abnormal/disturbed emotions and motives $\langle e^*/m^* \text{-- --}\rangle$ also.

DESTROYING THE AFFECT AND COGNITIVE SUPPORT SYSTEMS OF MPAs AND SIMs

Problem of overcoming human misery may now be posed in terms of destroying the cognitive frame and/or the affect configurations of MPAs and SIMs. Logically, the most proximate causal factors precipitating MPAs and SIM$_s$ are the drives and pressures of $\langle e^*/m^* s\rangle$. Hence the first approach toward eliminating human misery would appear to be a mitigation and/or neutralization of $\langle e^*/m^* s\rangle$ of MPAs and SIM$_s$. This solution approach thence directs a search for one or more such affect operators, $a_1, a_2, \ldots\ldots\ldots a_m$, as may weaken and/or nullify selectively or universally, high levels of $\langle e^*/m^* s\rangle$ like anger, hatred, greed, lust, bitterness, revenge, despair, hopelessness, and so on.

On the basis of reflective reasoning and testing for counter examples, two affect operators capable of nullifying $\langle e^*/m^* s\rangle$ are identified. They are independent of one another, and each of them by itself may smother and nullify abnormal emotions/motives in human minds. These two operators and (i) a Universal Love orientation toward all men and (ii) a state of Inner Calm/Peace i.e., mental equanimity in face of pleasure and pain, gain and loss, triumph, and tragedy.

These two affect operators differ in their nature and mode of operation. Love operator, for example, implies an universal attitude of goodwill, charity, kindness, and benevolence, towards all men irrespective of their race, religion, language, creed, community and nationality. This attitudinal orientation also logically carries over to action. Love in action i.e., selfless service, becomes a governing principle of conduct. Its other corollaries at behavioural level are: humility and courtesy, sensitivity to needs and feelings of others, and refraining from ill will and malice in thought, word, and deed. Lover operator thence not only does not allow abnormal (e^*/m^* s) to grow in human mind, but also weakens them at its behavioural level. An individual possessed by love would be incapable of carrying out any MpA.

Affect operator of Inner Calm implies cultivation and steady state maintenance of mental equanimity amidst situations of pressures, anxieties, and emotional turmoil. At conational level, this operator implies that an actor keeps himself detached i.e., emotionally uninvolved in results in his actions. He adopts perspective of a witness toward consequences of his own actions. Actions themselves are done as duty and unselfish service to fellowmen. Under such a stance of affect and conation, MpAs are ruled out.

Love and Inner Calm, though analytically independent are mutually compatible and supportive. There is no logical or empirical contradiction involved in their conjoint presence in human mind. But as mentioned earlier, any one of them by itself is capable of nullifying sets $< e^*/m^*, \ldots\ldots\ldots \geq$, and thence preventing emergence of MpAs and/or SIMs.

The two affect operators are equally effective in cases of self-induced states of misery (SIM_s) of mental diseases and suicide. Love orientation here serves to protect a vulnerable person's social bonds so that he does not become a rootless social isolate. Inner Calm operator serves to protect his ego from disruptive impacts of frustrations and anxiety neurosis. Hence a vulnerable person is enabled to escape the trap of self- reinforcing psychological disturbances, and their build up into crises of identity, alienation, anomie and despair.

COGNITIVE BASES OF NULLIFYING AFFECT OPERATORS

Above solution approach to problem of human misery is however, essentially incomplete. Neutralization of motive sets $< e^*/m^*, \text{——} >$ by two nullifying affect operators blocks any emergence of MpAs in thoughts and actions of men. SIMs are also blocked off effectively. But a basic issue i.e., how to sustain the affect operators, remains. In terms of consistency requirement, the affect dimension of human action has to be matched by its corresponding cognitive dimension. Hence, identification of compatible and matching cognitive frame(s) for steadily sustaining the affect states of Universal Love and Inner Calm becomes necessary. In absence of matching cognitive frame(s), the required affect states would be non-maintainable on their own. Cognitive bases of Love and Inner Calm operators are sought to be identified in what follows.

(1) THE UNIVERSAL LOVE (UL) OPERATOR

Every person including a brutal criminal is capable of love sentiments toward some. Behaviour of a loving person is directed toward making his loved one(s) happy. He gets joy by pleasing loved person(s). Love orientation may be instinctive as in case of one's family, close kinsmen, and fast friends. Or, it may be reflective i.e., based on one's reciprocation of sympathy and kindness of others.

Universal Love operator signifies expansion of love toward all persons. This operator thence required cognitive basis on which a love relationship with all men may in principle be possible. Since a person cannot love all others by receiving and reciprocating their kindness and sympathy, the only other basis for his universal love is the bond of kinship. The latter is again an apparent impossibility.

Belief in a Supreme Creator who loves all men as His children, however, makes the kinship bond realizable in principle. All persons become related to one another through their common descent from the Divine. All men become brothers through their common fatherhood in a Loving God. Promise of a loving supreme creator then provides a basic cognitive foundation for sustaining and maintaining a 'love all' orientation on a steady state basis. In absence of such a premise, conflict orientation would prevail in social systems as a natural corollary of man's competitive striving for scarce material values. In absence of Loving God, humans have no basis to be kind and sympathetic to one another, apart from momentary consideration of narrow self-interest.

No appeal is made here for the existence of a Supreme Creator on the basis of regularity, pattern, purpose, and design, in Nature. Discussion here is confined to the inference that for universal love orientation to exist in the minds of men, belief in a Supreme Loving

Creator is unavoidable. An alternative appeal to man's sense of kinship is on the basis of his belonging to a single biological species of Homo Sapiens. It however, is inherently weak. Doctrines of 'natural selection' and 'survival of the fittest' are integral parts of the Darwinian theory of evolution. Impact of these doctrines on human thought has been very unhealthy. It has resulted in theories of racial superiority, 'master' race(s), and superfluous 'inferior' races. Such theories have led to human strife, racial discrimination, oppression of ethnic groups, and deaths of hundreds of thousands in the Second World War.

THE PESSIMISM OF SOCIAL SCIENCES

Observations of Sociology, Political Science, and Social Psychology, also portray a gloomy picture of human group behaviour in this context. According to these social sciences, existence of an enemy is vital for strengthening the identity, unity and solidarity of human group. Presence of an enemy, and a state of conflict, are essential for promoting and sustaining internal cooperation within a group. Human groups trying to strengthen their identity and unity must then recurrently engage in conflict and enmity with other groups. A 'conflict model' in sociology goes even further. It views human society as operating in an ubiquitous mode of conflict and "the basic condition for social life is dissension, arising through the competition for power and advantage between the two groups" (Inkeles, 1954: 38-39). In Marxian theory of society, 'conflict between the two classes' is a central feature of social life, till an utopian 'classless' social order is eventually established. If these perspectives are carried to their logical conclusion, then mankind is forever doomed to conflict and misery. Tensions, antagonisms, violence, and destruction, consequently are inevitable in society. Men, women, and children, must continue to suffer privations and death, as long as, the mankind itself survives. Such social science 'findings' may scarcely be expected to provide a cognitive basis for Universal Love and elimination of human misery.

THE ONLY BASIS FOR THE UL OPERATOR

The common divine heritage that binds man to God, provides the basis for Love as the guiding light for humanity. The realisation that God/Divinity resides in every one, leads to the moral imperative that human beings should respect, love and help each other irrespective of caste, colour, and creed. Love thence provides the basis for individuals' self-directed mental and behavioural transformation. The latter would in turn lead mankind toward a 'single caste of humanity' conversing in an 'universal language of the heart'. Love, compassion, kindness, and sympathy at the level of thought and action are capable of removing all causes, sources, barriers and provocations of class, caste, creed, colour, and race. Love is capable of replacing existing suspicion, hate and violence among men, groups, and nations, with mutual kindness and harmonious cooperation[4]. The evangel of love provides mankind a radical alternative to present escalation toward co-destruction.

(2) THE INNER CALM OPERATOR

Identification of a matching cognitive frame for affect operator of Inner Calm/Peace is also an involved issue. Focal point here is: why should a person remain emotively unaffected by events, men, and situations that he encounters every day? External developments may affect him in varying ways ranging from peripheral concern to vital personal stakes. His emotional reactions to harm/benefits, joy/sorrow, loss/gain are but 'natural;. On what rational ground(s) should he then remain serene?

An *apriori* ground on which a man may justify his serenity amidst environmental changes is the inherent non- importance of worldly matters and men. It is not worthwhile to get excited and incur emotional strain over transient things. Cognitive premises supporting an affect state of inner calm/equanimity may thence be stated as follows:

(1) Non-importance of worldly concerns arises from man's own mortality and death being the end point of a short sequence beginning at birth. Man's material possessions, achievements, and life, are all transitory and evanescent in the Cosmos. One's wealth, cherished persons, and valued objects, are all left behind after one's death. In the light of these facts, why should one get sorely upset over persons, events, and things, of this world?[5]

(2) Human existence is not confined to gross human body which is subject to disease and death. According to scriptures, man possesses an imperishable soul (*atma*) which is an innate part of the Divine Being (*Parmatma*). Foremost

purpose of a man's life is thence to realize his unity with the Divine. In the light of such a spiritual goal, pleasures and pains, gains and losses, joys and sorrows of the world, are seen to be not important enough to disrupt/destroy one's inner tranquility and repose.

(3) Man's true nature is that of an *atma*. He is hence, in effect, just a witness of events and his actions. He is a detached observer living and participating in the world, but is not of the world. His true identity is that of oneness with the Divine, and which thus transcends his diverse social roles in society. There is thence no basic reason for him to be neurotically perturbed over persons, situation, and events of a phenomenal world.

These cognitive premises are compatible with those of the Universal Love operator. They in fact serve to elaborate man's transcendental relationship.

Burden of reasoning here is not a truth-value assessment of the above cognitive premises. Man's divine connection for example, cannot be investigated through man's sensory apparatus. It, however, is a fact that basic non-ritualistic teachings of major world religions in this context, are congruent. They are reflected in the cognitive premises of the two affect operators outlined here. Discussion and reasoning are here oriented toward finding a solution approach for the problem of human misery. In this connection, man is seen to need the cultivation and maintenance of the two affect states. In order to do so, he however, needs a compatible and matching belief system that may sustain the two affect states, in a logico-rational manner. Premises comprising such a belief system require existence of a Supreme Creator, and man's relationship of identity with him. These premises are seen to be needed for a systematic approach to the misery problem. They are not extraneous to the problem's structure.

If a misery-less social existence be a basic goal of mankind, then the above nexus of belief system, and affect states, would appear to be an intrinsic requirement for leading social systems toward that goal. Premises of the belief system, and the need of maintaining the two affect states, have to be internalized by men in their social interaction. Social interaction by men with strengthened personality systems would then usher in a misery-free, joyous, social existence.

VIOLENCE, STRUGGLE FOR PUBLIC CAUSES AND DUTY

Affect operators of Universal Love, and Inner Serenity, and their supportive cognitive premises, should not be interpreted to imply man's total abnegation of force and violence in legitimate pursuit of his duties. A policeman dealing with armed criminals, a judge sentencing a murderer to death, a public prosecutor demanding exemplary punishment for dowry crimes, and an army man fighting for his country, are a few examples where violence against others is involved in the very concept of one's duty.

Duty involving force and violence, done in a detached and honest manner, and in a spirit of unselfish service, is in accordance with righteous conduct. If however, the actors in such situations, hate and detest their victims, enjoy use of force and violence for sadistic pleasure, are vain and irresponsible, then their actions would be indistinct from M_pAs. Duty orientation here implies hating the crimes and evils, but not the criminals and evil doers as individuals. Men are expected to do their work sincerely, competently, and without vanity and greed, in accordance with their station in life. Duty involving force and violence, done in the above manner, would not be inconsistent with the two affect operators, for hate/revenge/greed/vanity of M_PAs are not the motive(s) for action here.

In another class of situations, men of ideals and convictions may be seen to devote their lives to protracted struggles against colonial rule; oppression of weak, exploitation of poor, evils of dowry, untouchability, communal hatred, racial discrimination, and so on. They may carry on a life-long struggle as a part of their self-conceived moral duty. Universal Love, and Inner Calm, here do not imply loving oppressors, evil doers, and exploiters, and calmly ignoring misery and sufferings of oppressed and exploited human beings[6]. What the affect operators do imply is that the focus of struggle(s) should be on eliminating evils and maladies, and not the persons. There should be no spirit of hate, revenge, anger, and bitterness. Opportunities for change of outlook and heart of wrong-doers should be provided and created. Struggle itself should be carried out in a spirit of unselfish service to suffering humanity. Emotive orientations of universal love and inner serenity do not make a person insensitive and unresponsive to needs for fighting injustice, exploitation, oppression, and evils. They do however, make a significant difference in the manner of carrying out such a struggle, and the nature of basic goals sought to be achieved through it.

FRAMEWORK OF SOLUTION

This chapter has tried to show that misery is produced and emitted in human interaction. The sources of this ubiquitous pollution lie in the minds of men themselves. Those who execute MPAs and/or are in SIM$_s$ are afflicted in mind. This inference is in accord with the UNESCO preamble, ---- 'Since wars begin in the minds of men, it is in the minds of men that defences of peace must be constructed'. Solution of the problem thence in principle requires a self-directed, and socially supported change, in the cognitive world-view and affect states of socii in interaction.

Problem of misery is then approached from the vantage-point of abnormal and disturbed emotions/motives (e^*/m^*s) as the most proximate causal factors of MPAs and SIMs. Nullification of sets $<e^*/m^*, ...>$ is rendered possible by the two affect operators. Congnitive frame for sustaining the affect states of two operators is seen to require the following premises of belief:

(P1) Existence of a Supreme Creator of men and Cosmos;

(P2) Kinship of man through their common source in the Divine;

(P3) Non-paramountsy of wordly matters and things due to their transient and perishable nature, and man's own mortality, and

(P4) The unity and identity of man with the Divine.

These premises of belief have to be internalised as truth (*Sathya*) by man before they may regulate his emotions/motives and behaviour. They cognitively match the affect states of Universal Love (*Prem*) and Inner Calm (*Shanthi*). Cognitive frame (*Sathya*) and matching affect states (*Prem* and *Santhi*) lead to righteous actions (*Dharma*) as opposed to MPAs. SIM$_s$ are also overcome by the two affect states. Both MPAs and SIM$_s$ are thus eliminated from thoughts and deeds of transformed persons. Truth (Sathya), Love (Prem), Serenity (Shathi), and Righteous Action (Dharma), may be viewed as a set of *super rational values* which is valid for all men, everywhere in the world.

Conflict and misery constitute a noxious sociological pollution of human social systems. The solution framework here focuses on changing an individual's existing preference/utility/goal structure toward a super-ordinate one of realising his Divine nature and destiny. Four superrational values of Truth, Love, Serenity, and Righteous Actions define his new frame of reference. New spiritual/transcendal goal and beliefs, values and vision, replace the pre-existing ones in the individual's personality system. They govern his thinking, feeling, and action, in correlated and mutually supportive manner.

CONCLUSION

The search for a steady state solution to the problems of ethnic schisms and national integrations, is seen to be embedded in the search for solution to the wider problem of human misery and suffering in society. The basis of solution lies in realizing the common identity of all human beings every where through their intrinsic kinship with the Divine. It lies in the realization of their 'Unity in Divinity'. It thence constitutes a most basic, in-depth, and permanent solution to the problem of ethnic schisms and conflicts. It replaces the 'Perceived Ethnic Basis of Self- Identity by Individuals' by 'perceived Common Divine Basis of self-identity by individuals', under the new dispensation. Sustained, long term, and dedicated cultivation of man's common identity would however, not only eliminate ethnic tensions, but also simultaneously overcome the problems of crime, exploitation, oppression, mental illness, social strife, and war. It would thence bring about a miseryless and joyous social order based on man's communion with the Divine.

References

1. Men suffer in society due to a wide variety of factors—administrative, economic, political, psychological, religio-cultural and social. Moore (1972; 2) however restricts the consideration of human misery to political factors only. He considers (i) war, (ii) poverty, (iii) injustice and oppression and (iv) persecution for dissident beliefs, as the primary causes of human suffering. The perspective adopted here is much broader and Moore's 'causes' are here broadly termed as misery - producing acts (MpAs). In accordance with his focus on political factors only, Moore provides following limited classification of misery experiences: (1) being tortured or slaughtered by a cruel enemy; (2) starvation and illness; (3) the exactations of ruthless authorities who carry off the fruits of

prolonged labour; (4) the loss of beloved persons through the acts of others over which one has little or no control; and (5) rotting in prison, being burned at the stake, or even simply losing the means of livelihood for the expression of heretical of unpopular beliefs (*ibid.*, p.2).

2. Moore in this connection emphasizes that, 'the general role of cruelty, --- is to sustain or to subvert and overthrow a specific social order. He also links the historically observed phenomenon of large scale cruelty with 'the struggle to establish or prevent the establishment of historically specific institutions such as Christianity, feudalism, capitalism, liberal democracy, socialism ---, (*Ibid.*, 24).
   He thus ignores wide prevalence of mental and physical cruelty in brutal decoities; kidnapping of victims for sexual abuse or torture or ransom; harassment of brides for dowry; threats of blackmail; terror tactics of mobsters; street muggings and tortures by young thugs ('teddy boys'); 'enforcement' activities of criminal syndicates; and a general milieu of insensate and cruel violence in many rural hamlets and urban slums.
3. Perception of victim(s) as an object is also highlighted by Jordan (1969, 183-184; 233-234) in the context of other MpAs. He points out that in cases of lynch mobs or fascist guards beating and bullying concentration camp prisoners, the perpetrators of cruelty define the victim as in some way non-human, or not quite human.
4. Importance of love in dealing with problems of antagonistic relations between ethnic communities is highlighted by a Pakistani social scientist. He analyses the historical and contemporary situation of Muslim communities in South-East Asian countries including India. After referring to Muslims own role in engendering inter-communal, political and economic problems facing them, he is led to recognize the importance of love and goodwill on their part in resolving the community's problems. He, in this connection, advocates the adoption of a motto of medieval Sufi Saints, *'sulh-i-kul'*, i.e., peace and goodwill toward all, by the Muslim communities presently rocked with hate, rage, and despair (Ahmad, 1982). Needless to say, the validity and relevance of his suggestion is not confined to Muslims alone. The evangel of love is universal.
5. Buddhism adopts a stronger position in this context. Here, the state of inner calm/mental tranquility is related with a psychic state of 'desirelessness'. Such a mental state is to be cultivated by a person who wants to be free from misery. Desires are viewed as sources of sorrow and unhappiness. An enlightened and liberated person is thence one who has become desireless.
6. *Githa*, the ancient Indian scriptural text, provides a classic example of a mistaken Love orientation coming in the way of warrior prince Arjun's duty to fight his kinsmen and elders for his rights. Lord Krishna, through His teachings enjoins Arjuna to do his duty (*dharma*) of fighting usurpers and oppressors, as part of man's duty to struggle against injustice and oppression.

APPENDICES

Appendix I

PROGNOSIS OF SIKH TERRORISM IN PUNJAB

Beginning of the eighties saw the emergence of a politics of terror in Punjab. It centres around the demand for an 'independent' Sikh nation. This politics of violence expresses itself in symbols of Sikh religion and ethnicity. Places of religious worship (*gurudwaras*) became sites of militant political mobilization, storehouse of arms, camps of heavily armed militants, and sanctuaries of terrorists and criminals.

The Sikh terrorists have killed thousands of innocent persons. They include political leaders, journalists, public figures, police personnel, Government employees, Hindu priests, members of Nirankari community, and common citizens—men, women, and children. Hindu temples have been defiled, damaged, and burnt. Indian planes were hijacked to Pakistan. Scores of bomb attacks on public places continue to be made in abid to intimidate the goverment, and terrorize the Hindus. Repeated massacres of bus and train passengers continue to occur. The Akali Sikh political leaders have not only refused to condemn the perpetrator of these heinous acts, but have also often perversely accused the Government of 'creating' these incidents to malign the Sikhs. To complete this bizarre picture, the Akali leaders have also been accusing the Central Government of gross and continuing discrimination against the Sikhs, of keeping the Sikhs in 'slavery', and calling upon the Sikh masses to prepare for and engage in, a prolonged 'holy' armed struggle (*dharma yudh*) for their 'honour' and independence.

The continuing imbroglio has engendered increasing social distance, communal tensions, and angry riots between the Sikhs and the Hindus.

Origins of the crisis may be traced back to 1947 when the British ruled Indian subcontinent was partitioned into two nations of India and Pakistan.[7] The Sikh leaders at that turning point in history, desired an independent nation of their own. Owing to the constraints of the then prevailing situation, they however, decided to remain in the Indian Union.

As part of the Union, the Sikh community during the last four and a half decades has emerged as the most affluent of all the ethnic groups. They have prospered in agriculture, industry, business, services, politics, and professions, all over the country.[89] The vision of an independent religio-cultural and politico-economic identity for the community has, however, continued to bestir the orthodox Sikh leadership in the context of their internally competitive ethno-politics. This vision has led the Sikh leaders to recurrently engage in mass agitations for securing communal previleges designed to promote their politico-economic, and religio-cultural interests. The alternative to these mass agitations according to them, would be the loss of the Sikh's distinctive identity in course of time. Under the influence of modernizaion, the Sikhs may gradually be assimilated into the larger Hindu society with which they share the historic ties of religion and kinship.[10] Mass agitations and continuing propaganda of discrimination against the Sikhs, serve the function of strengthening communal consciousness besides providing the Akali politicians with importance and recognition. The Sikh masses, moreover have always displayed their readiness to be mobilized for what they regard as the cause of defending their honour, religion, and culture.

The process of recurrent agitaions led to the creation of regional councils in 1956, Punjabi universities in the sixties, and Punjabi suba in 1967. After attaining the latter, Sant Fateh Singh declared that it was the 'last' political demand of the Sikhs. He was to be proved wrong after only five years.

In 1973, the then Akali Dal passed the Anandpur Sahib Resolution' demanding the recognition of Sikhs as a separate nation. By late seventies, a small section of educated Sikhs raised the demand for an independent Sikh state of **Khalistan.** According to them, only in an independent homeland of their own, could the Sikhs protect their religion, culture, economic rights, and collective identity. All along the last four decades, the Sikh leaders have kept up the refrain of gross discrimination against the Sikhs. According to Bhindranwale, the Sikhs have been kept as 'slaves' in India. G.S. Tohra has talked of the genocide of Sikhs and the entire Sikh Panth turning extremist. For these reasons, the Punjab must be turned into a state where the **Khalsa** will rule (**khalse ka bol bala**). The extremists want to unite the Sikh masses for an armed struggle by fomenting Hindu-Sikh communal conflict, terrorizing the Hindu population into leaving the state or submission, and making Punjab ungovernable for the Indian Government.

On account of the continuance of large scale violence by the Sikh terrorists, and repeated failures of the government to reach an understanding with the Akali Dal, alongwith the latter's latest move to stop the flow of foodgrains, water, and power, from Punjab to the neighbouring states, the army was called in to tackle the situation on June 3, 1984. By June 6, the army acting in a very restrained manner, had cleared the Golden Temple of the extremists. The army simultaneously flushed out the extremists in 38 other *gurudwaras* and a mosque in the state. Some 250 extremists were killed and over 1100 along with a huge stock of arms and ammunition captured. Army lost some 60 men. The first phase of the army's operation was over. The solution of the problem has however, remained remote.

The second phase of army operation commenced from 1990. Besides army, the units of Border Security Force (BSF), and the Central Reserve Force (CRPF), were also stationed in the State. Government's repeated efforts to seek a political solution to the problem of insurgency and terrorism, have failed. The erstwhile Akali Dal, has splintered into several factions. The leaders of these factions are mortally afraid of the heavily armed extremists. The resource base of the latter is large. They receive arms and money, training and sanctuary from Pakistan, and Sikh organizations in Western countries. Throughout the period of last decade and till today (1992), their disruptive activites of terror, violence, and destruction, have continued unabated.

The present problem in Punjab is not a problem of peaceful agitation for power by the Sikh political parties of leaders. The problem is essentially that the insurgency by a section of the Sikhs, of the factors underlying it, the factors sustaining it, the consequences emanating from it, and the consequences generated by its persistence and growth.

EMPIRICAL EXPLICATION OF THE SYSTEM VARIABLES

In what follows, the variables of the problem's generic model(Fig. 4) are briefly discussed one by one. Each variable is explicated empirically in respect of the situational details of the Sikh extremism problem.

1. Process of Socio-Cultural Change and Modernisation

This variable here refers to the processes of increasing urbanization, industrialization, spread of western ideas and culture, population growth, pressure on land, competitiveness of modern economic life, role of education, science and technology in the economy, and emigration of the Sikhs to other places and countries. These changes have affected the Sikh community concentrated mostly in Punjab. The change processes have jointly and severally destabilized their traditional bases of life and self-identification. They have generated pressures that compel adjustment on the part of the persons and the community.

Punjab has been undergoing rapid socio-cultural and politico-economic change over the last several decades. These changes have created pressures and anxieties for the individuals and the groups, to redefine their traditional roles, goals, values, and identity in a dynamic milieu.

2 and 3. Requirements of Adjustment to Pressures of Change; and Problems of Identity, Insecurity and Politico-Economic Interests

For the Sikh community in Punjab, the stresses of change have primarily been psycho-social, and socio-cultural, rather than economic. Economically, the Sikhs have been very successful, and are the most affluent community in the country. But the spread of modern thoughts, ideas, and cultural influences, have presented serious threats to Sikh traditions and culture. Young men began to shave their beards, smoke, drink and show indifference toward religious rituals and symbols in the sixties. Clean shaven Sikhs i.e., the Hindus respecting the teachings of Sikh gurus provided the Sikh young men with a syncretic model through which they could escape beard and turban without severing their family and communal bonds. These trends alarmed the community's leaders, and they genuinely began to fear the possibility of their small community's disappearance through assimilation in the larger Hindu fold. This perhaps is one of the reasons behind the inveterately hostile utterances of some Sikh leaders against the Hindus.

Fear of the future brought before the Sikh leaders, the problems of sharply defining, distinguishing, and preserving, their ethno-cultural group identity. In the event of their failure to do so, the community in their opinion would for ever lose its glorious religio-cultural heritage, and be reduced to the status of self-serving ordinary middle class Hindus. Anxieties concerning the preservation of communal identity, and psychological insecurities concerning its maintenance and survival, have among other factors, governed the political responses of the Sikh leaders in the post-Independence period. Their efforts have invariably been guided by the concern to emphasize and promote their separate communal identity through a graduated series of demands. These demands have ranged from linguistic rights in the beginning to autonomy, separate nationhood, and an independent Sikh state as at present. Politico-economic interests of the community have been defined in terms of its sectarian demands, and judging from the success record of successive Sikh leaders in promoting their communal interests, this approach and strategy have served the community well. Attainment of sectarian politico-economic interests has become identical with their promotion and assertion of religio-cultural identity.

4. Perceived Ethnic Basis of Self-Identity by Individuals

Sikhs are ever conscious of their ethnic identity on account of their distinctive appearance. Each Sikh has to wear a turban, underwear and a steel bracelet, keep uncut hair including a beard and carry a sword (five 'K's). These things are enjoined upon him by compulsory religious rituals. Gurdwaras as places of worship, social ceremonials, and religio-political discourses; use of religion both as a guide to conduct and political ideology; worship of arms and the use of Punjabi in *gurumukhi* script; are a few other communal features designed to stress their distinctive ethnic identity. The socialization and life-experiences of the Sikhs in various ethno-social institutions reinforce the ethnic basis of their self-perception as social individuals. Their high social visibility serves as a built-in factor promoting their communal consciousness.

5. Attitudes, Beliefs and Perception of Interests Corresponding to Ethnic Group Identity

Consciousness of their distinctive ethnic identity by individuals, leads them to develop attitudes, beliefs and ideas reflecting the collective interests of their own ethnic group. Accordingly for the Sikhs, their language, religion, culture, economic and political interests become their 'natural' standards and criteria for judging various issues, events and matters. An exclusive concern with the promotion of their community's rights and interests becomes the rationale and over-riding objective behind Sikh leader's formulation of their politico-economic demands.

Episodes of historical glory become the inspiration behind the pursuit of goals for communal aggrandizement. The lofty heights of the Sikh gurus, the supreme sacrifices and dedication of Guru Gobind Singhji, and politico-military glory of the great Maharaja Ranjit Singhji, are held out as the sources of inspiration for the arousal of communal frenzy. In terms of such a circumscribed world view, the demands for a separate national identity for the Sikhs sound very logical and reasonable to the Sikh masses. The views and interests of other groups do not find a place in their perception, thought and action. Their weltanschauung is characterized by its self-closure.

6. Organization(s) for the Affirmation of Ethnic Identity and Promotion of Group Interests

Two foremost official Sikh organizations are the Shiromani Gurdwara Prabandhak Committee (SGPC) and the Akali Dal. The latter has now been split into several factions. The SGPC is concerned with the management of Sikh gurdwaras including the Golden Temple and their resources. Its primary ostensible role is religio-cultural. Its annual budget runs into several crores of rupess. It runs several educational and charitable institutions for the Sikhs and employs thousands of persons as preachers, guards and servitors. The SGPC president and members play an influential role in Sikh politics. The former united Akali Dal was primarily concerned with the politico-economic interests of the Sikhs. It sponsored its own candidates for elections to state lelgislature, and Parliament from Sikh dominated constituencies. It also entered into electoral alliances with other political parties for forming Government in Punjab. The Dal had a symbolic relationship with the SGPC. Its linkage with the rural masses and the latter's mobilization for agitation(s), were effected through its jathedars (group leaders) drawn from various villages. These 'jathedars seen in the Hindu-Sikh amity a mortal threat to their stranglehold over the affairs of the Sikh Community'.[11]

There are also various other socio-cultural organizations of the Sikhs at local and state levels. Sectarian Sikh organizations like those of students, teachers, lawyers, women, and ex- servicemen are also active. But, by an large, the primacy of the SGPC, and Akal Takht are recognized by the Sikhs all over India. Another major organization is All India Sikh Students Federation (AISSF). It is also divided into several factions at present. Anandpur Sahib Resolution of 1973 is reportedly based on the ideas espoused by the AISSF in the fifties. Its members are known to be widely engaged in the extremist activities. The AISSF periodically organized secret camps for the indoctrination and 'advanced' training in arms for the Sikh youth.

Over half-a-dozen underground extremist organizations besides the AISSF have emerged since the late seventies. They are variously known as Khalistan Commando Force (KCF), Khalistan Liberation Force (KLF), Babbar Khalsa, Bhindranwale Tiger Force (BTF), and Dashmesh Regiment, etc; Their activities are governed by 'Panthic Committees', whose leaders in most cases live in Pakistan. All of them are heavily armed with sophisticated weapons, and had earlier their headquarters at the Golden Temple. Official Sikh leadership apprehends its eclipse, impeachment, and elimination by the extremists and the hardliners, in the event of a compromise settlement with the Government that does not have their approval.

7. Sectarian Socio-Political Orientation of Group Members

Development of a marked communal socio-political orientation amongst the Sikhs is an empirically observable logical consequence of the interaction of the preceding variables. It denotes their natural tendency to give primacy to Sikh interests in their perception, thought, and action. It also correlatively denotes the tendency of the Sikh masses to get emotionally disturbed and agitated over what they are told about the 'dangers' to their religion and culture. Over the last four decades they have been recurrently mobilised for political agitations by their leaders' effective use of the religious symbols and themes in their propaganda. This variable thence also signifies a relatively closed world view of the community and its leadership.

Akali leaderships' ambivalence in unequivocally condemning the massacres of innocent unarmed Hindus by the extremists, indicates a high level of their communal fanaticism. The extremist leaders like Bhindranwale encouraged and glorified such wanton atrocities and their perpetrators. Such insensitivity on their part to human misery and suffering, and glorification of senseless violence, attests to the strength and rigidity of sectarian socio-political orientation of a large section of the Sikhs and their leaders.

8. Perceived Grievances and Deprivation of Ethnic Group Members

Sustained propaganda over the years by the Akali leaders about alleged discrimination against the Sikhs, and a devaluation of their importance and identity, has generated amongst the Sikh masses feeling of disaffection. The Sikhs received a differentially previleged treatment from the British in the matter of their recruitment for Government services, and the armed forces. These discriminatory previleges are no longer available to them as a community in the Indian democracy. But empirical data consistently indicates their predominance in every field of life in Punjab, and prosperous socio-economic status in other parts of the country. The main grievance propagated by the 'moderate' Akali leadership concerned the acceptance of their 'autonomy' demand by the Centre, in terms of the Anandpur Sahib Resolution. Their ambition for a Sikh dominated Punjab also led the Akali leaders to demand the disenfranchisement of the emigrant Hindu farm workers in Punjab on the ground that they do not own property in the state. Persistent religio-ethnic propaganda has changed the perceptions of the Sikh masses toward secessionist aspirations. "In the minds of rural groups there are dreams that the Sikhs will rule again as a religious power" (Rustamji , 1983; p. 45).

The Anandpur Sahib Resolution in essence demands a semi-independent Sikh nation as mentioned earlier. The extremists demand outright independence. The fact that most of the Akalis have consistently continued to support the extremists' activities, and the extremists have continued their campaign of murders, massacres, and dacoities, show that the real 'grievances' of the Akalis are their secessionist communal aspirations.

9. Political Expression of Sectarian Demands

This has taken the form of highly provocative propaganda against the Government and the Hindu community through ethnic media, religious congregations, and **gurdwara** premises. The evolution of the political expression of sectarian demands has moved away from **morchas** (mob confrontations and militant demonstrations), **bandhs** (strikes), and blockades of rail and road transport, to wanton killings for terror, massacres,kidnappinngs, looting of public funds, and assassinations of political figures and journalists. The resource base of the extremists in terms of arms, money, information sources, and infrastructure, is wide and strong. The capacity of the extremist groups to wage a continuous war of low intensity, and organized insurgency, is high. It has remained undiminished despite the government's armed action, so far. The involvement of Pakistan in building up the armed capabilities and disruptive potential of the Sikh insurgents has been, and remains deep.

10. Reactions of Other Groups

They have taken the form of growing fear, despair, and insecurity among the Hindus of Punjab, and anger and hate amongst the Hindus of Haryana, and the neighbouring states. A number of Hindu organization meant for protecting the Hindu lives, property, and politico-economic interests, have come up since 1982. Hindu reaction has largely been confined to demonstrations, processions, and strikes, protesting against the Government's failure to put down the extremists' violence and terror. Hindu-Sikh riots began to erupt from 1982 and increased in frequency in 1983 and 1984. In February 1984, extensive anti-Sikh riots occurred in several cities of Haryana followed by retaliatory killings by extremists in Punjab.

Extensive anti-Sikh riots against the murder of Mrs. Gandhi by her Sikh body guard occurred in Delhi and various parts of the country in 1984. Anti-Sikh sentiments have spread throughout the country.

At the cognitive level, the Hindus perceive the Akali emphasis on a separate religio-political identity for the Sikhs as insincere. They also question the validity of the Sikh fear of the loss of their distinctive identity. According to the Hindu view, "Sikhism has successfully grown on the Hindu body social", and identities are subject to change with time and circumstance. This view further refers to the fact that nine out of the ten Sikh Gurus were Hindu Khatris, none of whom was 'Singh'. Guru Govind Singh, who founded the Khalsa, did so with the clarion call:

Sakal jagat mahein Khalsa panth gajjay
Jagay dharma Hindu, sakal bhand bhaajay.
(May the Khalsa panth flourish all over the world. May Hindu Dharma awake and expose all falsehoods)

It is significant that Guru Gobind Singh was neither born in Punjab, nor died there. He was born in Patna, Bihar, and he died in Nanded, Maharashtra. He was a worshipper of Goddess Chandi, and has written more Hindi than Punjabi.

Maharaja Ranjit Singh established the Lahore Darbar on Divali 1761; he demanded that Afghanistan return the doors of Somnath, and willed the Kohinoor diamond to Jagannath Puri. When British rule came, hundred of Sikhs died for cow protection in the Kuka movement'.

11. Mutual Distrust and Tension

This variable here is an extension of the previous variable. Alienation between the Hindus and Sikhs has increased to an unprecedented level. High value of this variable from 1982 onward has recurrently manifested itself in the form of Hindu-Sikh communal tension, violence and riots. "The latest symbol of Hindu revivalism is the 'Trishul' just as sword or the gun is the symbol of Sikh revivalism. - - - - - More than 2000 Hindus in the city are reported to have applied for gun or rifle licences - - - - - They (Hindus) are no longer willing to take it lying down."[12] At the level of business and industry also, the tension and fear prevail. Social distance and mutual avoidance between the two communities have increased widely. Many Hindu families from rural areas of Punjab have emigrated to cities, and other parts of the country. In brief, the relations between both the communities have reached a blind alley.

12. Disturbed Law and Order Conditions

They have progressively worsened from 1981 onward. Initially the Akali morcha, and the sporadic killings of Nirankaris together presented a difficult situation. Increasing aggressiveness and escalation of Akali agitation were later paralleled by growing scope and violence of the extremists' activities. Administrative incompetence; political timidity; police ineffectiveness; infiltration of administration and police by the extremists and their sympathisers; the availablity of gurdwaras as protected base of operations by the extremists; demoralization of police due to kidnapping and selective killings of the police personnel, and members of their families; have together worsened the situation to such an extent that even massacres of Hindus are no longer a new development. Hindu-Sikh riots have further complicated the situation. Government's failure in tackling the situation at every stage of its development, has been its conspicuous feature so far.

13. Government's Armed Action

It has been singularly ineffective so far. Government has reacted to the worsening law and order conditions by making frequent changes in the police administration, and inducting additional security personnel in Punjab. Army units are now also parts of the regulatory effort. Its regulatory armed action has, however, been hampered by the extremists' infiltration of, and/or the presence of their sympathisers in the Punjab police and administration. The Government's timidity and inefficiency in the earlier stages rendered its armed action ineffective, and thence allowed the extremists to build up, and expand, their operations and infrastructure. The prevailing situation has acquired the dimensions of large scale insurgency in Punjab. The extremists' operations have spread over various points in the state. The range of their criminal activities presently also extends over areas of Haryana, U.P., and Rajasthan.

Failure of the Government's armed action is concomitant with the poor morale of the Punjab police, and the expansion of the terrorist activities and their infra-structure. "The loss of morale in the Punjab police is frightening - - - - - - the extremists have been killing the families of the policemen not sparing even the women and children - - - - - -. Only too often, it either does not risk making arrests, or having done so does not risk carrying out an investigation".[13]

14. Costs of Conflict

Costs of conflict so far, have been primarily incurred by the Hindus of Punjab, the Nirankaris, the banks, the loyal police personnel, and the Government. Some innocent Sikhs of Haryana have also lost their lives and property. The cost to the terrorists have been minimal. The extremists continue to remain rich, strong, and aggressive. The extremists' infrastructure, operations, and resources, not only have remained unaffected, they have in fact expanded. They have at most lost only some of their operatives. It is, therefore not surprising that the rebels remain unrelenting and disinclined towards ending their insurgency. They have no incentive to do so.

15, 16 and 17. Government's Assessment of Political Implications; Government's Policies; and Government's Responses

They have been faulty, confused, weak, and ineffective. The Government's intelligence machinery has been defective, its decisions tardy and timid, and its actions inadequate. It under estimated the menace of Sikh extremism, misjudged the long term real nature of Akali goals and fanaticism, failed to perceive the essential convergence of the objectives of the Akalis and the extremists, did not take strong and deterrent action against the terrorists from the beginning, and projected an image of weakness before the militants.

The Government perceived that the Akalis do not represent all sections of the Sikhs. They form only 30% of the mainly Jat Sikh population in the Punjab. But it apparently overlooked the vast resources and powers of patronage at the disposal of the Sikh organizations, the power and influence of the Jathedars, and their control of the highest seat of the Sikh religion, i.e., the Golden Temple. The income from gurdwaras is more than Rs. 200 crore per year. There are 12,000 villages in Punjab; from each village, these organizations can always draw fanatical volunteers for their holy war (**dharma yudh**). These volunteers receive regular training in arms, and indocrination in periodically organized secret camps.

The Government's dominant policy concerns have been to evolve a national consensus to deal with the Punjab problem by associating the opposition parties in negotiations with the Akalis, and avoid hurting the religious sentiments of the Sikhs. Both these concerns are related to its perception of its short term political interests. In the process, it has allowed hundreds of innocent Hindus, Nirankaris, and loyal police personnel, to be terrorized and murdered in cold blood. Instead of taking hard, adequate, and timely decisions and actions, to increase the costs of conflict to the terrorists and fanatics, and thence end the state of insurgency, it had been seeking soft options oblivious of the gravity of the extant situation, and its serious implications for nation's integrity

One of its basic policy assumptions has been regarding qualitative difference between the positions of the Akali leadership and the extremists. This assumption is erroneous in view of the historical and contemporary facts, and the nature of links between the extremists and the politicians. The only difference between the two is in their time schedule for the attainment of their secessionist aspirations. Even if the government reaches an agreement with the Dal leadership, two possibilities may arise. Under pressure from the growing strength of the extremists and the hardliners, they may not be able to implement it, and/or to save themselves from being impeached, repudiate it forthwith. Even if this does not happen and which is rather unlikely, there is nothing to prevent them from launching another agitation after some time for the acceptance of a more secessionist version of the Anandpur Sahib Resolution. In that case, the Government would have gained nothing, and the nation may face more serious problem from a weakened position.

A perceptible shift in the Goverments' hitherto weak and indecisive policies and responses occurred in 1984 following the continuing escalation of terrorist violence. The Government's realization that unless the extremists' activity was reduced, (i) it could not manage the state administration, (ii) control anti- Sikh riots in Haryana and elsewhere, and (iii) contain the growing resentment and frustration of the security personnel, may have also contributed to its later phase of a firmer stance against the extremists.

The phase of firmer action involved a quantum increase in the deployment of security personnel, short term imprisonment of hate-mongering Sikh politicians, and take over of the state administration by the Central Government. This phase had led to a decline in the level of insurgency, but the problem was far from over. Their requirements of a high level of competence, coordination, determination, and availability of high quality intelligence, have remained unmet in this context.

EXPLANATION OF THE PROBLEM

The dominant element of the situation here is the high value of the variable, Sectarian Socio-Political Orientation of Group Members. It has served to meet rather succesfully the Problems of Identity, Insecurity and Politico-Economic Interests of the Sikh community in Punjab. A high level of Sectarian Socio-Political Orientation inevitably generates a persistent sense of Perceived Grievances and Deprivation of Ethnic Group Members. Since economic factors in the deprivation of this affluent community are largely absent, the main exogenous impulse here is provided by the historical factors. Visions of the religio-cultural glory of the Khalsa rule, and ethno-political aspirations inspired by a sectarian interpretation of the community's history, serve to mobilize the Sikh masses for their realization as a long-term goal. This helps explain the graduated series of demands of the Akali leaders from the fifties onward to the present. Their cumulative purpose and direction has been toward securing a separate and autonomous political identity and nationhood for the Sikhs. Because of their economic resources, ambitions, and strength, the Jat Sikhs have been in the fore-front of the Sikh agitations.

Political Expression of sectarian demands has changed from the fifties. With the large increase in organizational resources in terms of men, money, arms, infrastructure, and influence; the internal ethno-political competition for the control of these vast resources, militancy, and fanaticism also increased. With the covert involvement of Pakistan in the situation, along with the growth of religious fundamentalism as a mode of adjustment to the pressures of modernization, and instrument for building up their leadership image by some ambitious Sikh leaders, the extremist politics of violence, terror, and secession, came to the fore in the late seventies. Its romanticism has caught the imagination of a large section of the Sikh youth. Escalating activities of the terrorist and confrontationist postures of the Akali leadership engendered tension, fear, insecurity, anger, and hate, amongst the Hindu leading to their retaliatory violence and communal riots. Ineffectiveness of the Government's armed action, policies, and responses; together with very low costs of conflict for the agitators and the extremists, have worsened the sitution and allowed its continuance and aggravation. In view of the continuing high values of the sectarian socio-political orientation of the Sikhs, the success pattern of their communal politics, and their vast organizational resources leading to militantly violent political expression of sectarian demands, and the high values of mutual distrust and tension between the Hindus and the Sikhs, the problem is not likely to end in the near future.

PROGNOSIS OF THE SITUATION

The most visible variable characterizing the present course of the Punjab problem is the Disturbed Law and Order Conditions. The following inferences focus on it and would thence easily be verifiable through empirical observations.

(1) If the Government is able to control the Disturbed Law and Order Conditions in an effective and sustained manner, it would thence be able to reduce the gravity of this problem. Control of Disturbed Law and Order Conditions, implies a complete elimination of the extremists' activities. Control of this variable would produce cascading changes through its linkages with other important system variables. The Government would thence also be able to reduce the disruptive political expression of sectarian demands, and the reactions of other groups(s).

(2) The Government would be able to effect improvements in the situation if it primarily focuses on increasing the Costs of conflict for the extremists to an unacceptable level. High costs of conflict together with continuing lack of success in achieving their goals, may serve to damage the morale of the insurgents.

(3) If the Government proves unable to effectively regulate the Disturbed Law and Order Conditions i.e., eliminate

riots, massacres, terrorism, attacks on banks, intimidation, and insurgency, then the situation may move toward a rather prolonged state of armed stalemate with resultant paralysis of the state's economy, administration, and orderly political processes. Continuing loss of Hindu lives and property may initiate their emigration from the state, along with a strengthening of organized Hindu communalism. Large scale expulsion of Hindus from Punjab is a major objective of the extremists. Correlatively, the Sikhs from Haryana and other parts of the country may emigrate to Punjab.

(4) The second contigency may also engender anti-Sikh riots in other states as part of the reactions of other group(s), to the continued killings of the Hindus in Punjab. The violence there would however, automaticallty subside as the situation improves in Punjab.

(5) Continuation of (3) if accompanied by severe national economic difficulties on account of an acute drought and/or subversive activities, may invite a more substantive covert/overt involvement of Pakistan and possibly other external powers in the disturbed situation. Such a contingency would markedly increase the level of politico-military pressure on the nation.

(6) The outcomes (3), (4) and (5) would also come about in the event of political instability and/or a weak government at the Centre. Under such conditions, the militancy of the Akalis and terrorism of the extremists may increase, and Pakistan may get more actively involved in promoting the secession of Punjab from India. Large scale killings of the Hindus may follow, and the secessionist activities in Kashmir may also increase as part of a coordinated action pattern by the enemies of the nation.

(7) If the Government accepts the autonomy and other demands of the communal Sikh leadership, then the following consequences may come to the fore:

   (i) Highly adverse reactions of other group(s) i.e., the Hindus in Punjab, Haryana, Himachal Pradesh, Rajasthan, and elsewhere, may generate serious politcal and agitational problems for the concerned State Governments, and an unacceptable electoral cost for the Congress (I) Party in many parts of the country.

(ii) All the non-Congress (I) State Governments and their political supporters may agitate together for transfer to them of the same autonomous powers as those granted to Punjab. Such a development would promote political fragmentation, and a weakening of the Central Government as an integrative mechanism.

(iii) With the consolidation of their political power and hold on the administrative machinery of the State, the Akalis may after sometime again come up with the demand for an independent Sikh nation. Political instability, and a weak Government at the Centre, would facilitate this development. This inference follows from the continuing high value of the variable, Sectarian Socio-Political Orientation of Group Members, and is supported by the historical course of the Akali politics.

(8) Persisting and increasing alienation between the Hindus and the Sikhs, and their growing communal polarisation would also increasingly communalise the Hindu and Sikh personnel in Punjab administration. Such a communalisation is in fact already in existence. Tensions and distrust between the Hindu and Sikh personnel in various organs of the State Government exist in varying degrees.

(9) If the official and non-official efforts to accuse the conscience of the non-fanatic Sikh masses against the terrorist killings of the innocent people, and effectively mobilise their public opinion succeed, they may help dampen the intensity of the communal schisms. If these efforts canalize toward the people's active cooperation with the official machinery in apprehending the terrorists and criminals, then the menace of terrorism and communal violence may be curbed. This, however, does not lessen the importance of sustained and effective implementation of both long and

short term measures by the government. The cumulative impact of the success of the non-official and official efforts would be to reduce the high value of the mutual distrust and tension variable, leading to a consequent improvement in the Disturbed Law and Order Conditions.

SUBJECTIVE WORLD VIEWS UNDERLYING ETHNIC SCHISMS

The inwards of the present problem lie in the sectarian socio-political Orientations of the Group Members of the two communities. Such an orientation of large sections of the Jat Sikh populace, continues to engender and sustain their sense of perceived grievances and deprivation. It also underlies the emergence and strengthening of mutual distrust and tensions between the two groups. It is therefore essential to understand the lineaments of the subjective world-views of the two communities in the present context. The subjective world-view of the extremist Sikhs, may be outlined as follows: It consists of their subjective beliefs, cultural aspirations, and historical images, and is an outcome of their indoctrination. It helps explain the subjective rationale of the extremists in carrying out their murderous and criminal activites without any compunction.

- Violence and terror are the necessary means for achieving the cherished goal.
- Purity of the Sikh faith, **Panth,** and Sikh identity, can be preserved only when the Sikhs are politically independent.
- The Government and the Hindus are weak and cowards; they can be brought to surrender if they are sufficiently terrorized. Sikhs are inherently superior to caste-ridden Hindus. Sikhs cannot live under Hindu domination.
- Terror against the Hindus is necessary for making them leave Punjab, as well as, mobilize the Sikhs.
- Pakistan, and China are sympathetic to the Sikh nation.
- Establishment of **Khalsa raj** is a historical necessity, the Sikhs have been making great sacrifices for it since the time of Guru Gobind Singhji.
- All anti-Panth elements inculding Nirankaris must be 'eliminated'.

- The Hindu Government at New Delhi has been 'exploiting' Punjab; without our foodgrains, they would starve.
- The Hindu government at New Delhi distrusts the Sikhs and discriminates against them. It is reducing the number of the Sikhs in army and does not promote Sikh officers. No Sikh has been appointed as the army chief.
- The Sikh armed personnel in the army and personnel are mostly with us.

THE SUBJECTIVE WORLD VIEW OF THE SIKH EXTREMISTS

The subjective world-view of the Hindus consists of their perceptions, beliefs, images, anxieties, fears, and apprehensions. Its lineaments may be outlined as follows. It helps explain the nature and rationale of the Hindu' responses to the unprecedented situation confronting them in Punjab.

- The Sikh Kaum (i.e., community) must have its glorious independent Khalsa nation.
- The Akalis and the extremists both want an independent Sikh state; only their tactics may differ.
- The extremists want to terrorize the non-Sikhs so that they may leave Punjab, or live under the Sikh domination as second class citizens.
- Government is weak and incompetent, and its policy of appeasement would only result in more deaths of the innocents. It has failed to protect the lives of innocent Hindus and Nirankaris.
- The extremists and their sympathisers have infiltrated the Punjab police, and the latter cannot be trusted.
- The Government should permit the armed forces to go anywhere and give them freedom of action for apprehending the criminals.
- Government has already given the Sikhs pre-eminance in every walk of life in Punjab, yet the latter are ever demanding more and more sectarian benefits.
- The Akali demands from time to time are just a prelude to their ultimate goal of an independent Sikh nation.
- It is essential for the Hindus and the Nirankaris to arm themselves, and organize for self-protection. Extremist criminals understand the language of force only.

- The extremists and the Akalis are not true followers of the Sikhism, and Guru Nanak's message of love and service.
- The Hindus have to exert collective pressure on the Government so that it does not surrender to the Akali fanatics and extremists.

THE SUBJECTIVE WORLD VIEW OF THE HINDUS

The world-view of the Hindus is characterized by their fears, anxieties, apprehensions, and distrust. It is, however, largely reactive, and has emerged as a consequence of the Sikh militancy. The two world-views together bring out the psychological miasma of distrust and distance that has developed between these two historically close communities.

TWO SITUATIONAL IMPERATIVES

The two imperative features of this situation are (i) the pathological cycle of *K* and *K'* factors, and (ii) the higly sectarian and competitive nature of the internal Sikh politics. The *K* and *K'* factors as mentioned in chapter 5, refer to a group's propensity to acquire and use arms, i.e., its high potential for recourse to violence in the pursuit of its ethno-political objectives. The self-reinforcing pathological cycle of these two factors is **hyper-active** in the present situation.

Unless and until, it is deactivated, expectations of any meaningful improvement in the situation, would be unrealistic. The second imperative feature is the highly fractious nature of the Sikh's internal politics in which the competition for power and leadership takes the form of continually amplifying the nature and expression of the group's sectarian demands. This competition by its very contextual nature relies on highly distorted visions of communal chauvinism and glory. This feature of the situation needs to be eliminated if the essence of the problem is to be tackled. The political role of the Sikh organizations thence requires to be re-defined if their potential for the propaganda of hate and separatisms is to be nullified.

If these two crucial features of this situation are controlled, the effectiveness of the long term solution measure would be greatly strengthened, and the close historical bonds of mutuality and harmony between the two communities revitalised.

References

1. For an account of the historical background of the Sikh's religio-political situation, see, Jones (1976), Menon (1968),Khushwant Singh (1953, 1966) Satinder Singh (1982), and Upreti (1982) among others. See also, G. Talwalkar, 'Search for a Sikh State—Akali Demand Before Partition', *The Times of India*, New Delhi, March 21, 1984.

2. For an account of the competing economic interests of the Hindus and Sikhs in Punjab, see D'Souza (1982). The following data however, serve to illustrate the dominance of the Sikhs in Punjab. Proportioh of Sikh population in Punjab according to 1981 census is 52% while the Hindus constitute the remaining 48%. Sikhs are mostly concentrated in the rural areas (over 70% of rural population) while the Hindus are concentrated in urban areas (over 67% of urban population). As against this population ratio, the Sikhs overwhelmingly predominate in every sector of Punjab's life. Out of 13 members of the then Parliament from Punjab, 10 were Sikhs; of the seven Rajya Sabha members, six were Sikhs; of the 117 MLAs, 84 were Sikhs; all the three vice- chancellors of state universities are Sikhs, and Sikh representation in university faculty, education department, economic departments, police and Government services varies from 80% to 90%. 'Samiti claims Sikhs enjoy top positions', *The Hindustan Times*, New Delhi, August 4, 1983.

3. For a perceptive sociological discussion of the Sikh's identity crisis, see M.V. Kamath, Spreading Violence: An Identity Crisis', *The Week*, March 11-17, 1984.

4. Satinder Singh, 'Sikh Politics', *The Economic Times*, Bombay, October 3, 1979, p. 5.

5. K.N. Khosla, 'Amritsar in a blind alley', *The Times of India*, New Delhi, March 16, 1984, p. 16.

6. P.S. Jha, 'Reaping the Whirlword—'The Fruits of the Soft State', *The Times of India*, New Delhi, April 2, 1984, p. 8.

APPENDIX II

PROGNOSIS OF THE HINDU-MUSLIM COMMUNAL TENSIONS IN THE COUNTRY

One of the most serious Hindu-Muslim communal riots in recent history—the Moradabad riots in 1980, were sparked off by a trivial incident. A pig belonging to a nearby scheduled caste family strayed into the Idgah prayer grounds after the Id prayers. Some of the Muslims who were armed began to attack the police personnel there after, and many of the latter were seriously injured. Additional District Magistrate was lynched to death. This incident which could have been dealt with as an ordinary problem calling for social censure, however, rapidly graduated towards extensive distrubances and violence in the city.

The disturbed situation which at one stage called for 'shoot at sight' orders, took several months before returning to normal.

The incident appears to have been engineered by the Muslim League communalists and Pakistani agents. "Hindu communalists among the citizens and the police force could have pushed the pig towards the Idgah. But surely they could not have ensured that some members of the congregation brought arms with them and used them to attack the police without the slightest hesitation. Those who were interested in creating the mischief had to be in a position to produce both the arms and the pig."[1]

Numerous observers of, and enquiry committee reports on, Hindu-Muslim communal conflicts have repeatedly emphasized the importance of timely and firm action in controlling the emerging situations of communal violence. It however, at best represents a short term attempt to minimize the seriousness of incipient and developing situations of violence by defusing them through timely measures. Unfortunately, the roots of the malaise lie deep, and these measures are not always quite appropriate. They lie in the deep rooted emotions of distrust, hate, rage, contempt, and bitterness of large sections of the two communities towards each other.[2] These emotions i.e., the affect states, are however, supported by matching cognitive world-views of the two communities towards one another. These congnitive world-views consist of a set of negative images, beliefs, stereotypes, and prejudices about the other community. They are from time to time reinforced by feelings of politico-economic and psycho-cultural insecurities engendered by contemporary socio- political events and developments.

EMPIRICAL EXPLICATION OF SYSTEM VARIABLES

System variables for this problem are briefly explicated in terms of their empirical details as follows. They together serve to clarify our understanding of this chronic problem. The focus of discussion is on the Muslims as a group.

1. Processes of Socio-Cultural Change and Modernization

The major process of change in the present context has been the country's struggle for independence from British rule, and for economic development there after. With the creation of Pakistan in 1947, Muslims in India found themselves as the largest minority in the Hindu-majority state of the Indian Union. Since Independence, the country has been trying hard to overcome its problems of poverty, illiteracy, backwardness, over population, regionalism, linguistic diversity, and lack of industrial infrastructure. For attaining these objectives, the country adopted the path of democracy, socialistic pattern, secularism, and indigenous development of scientific and technological capabilities. National efforts in these directions have however, been adversely affected by administrative weaknesses, population growth, and problems of defence engendered by conflicts with Pakistan and China.

As a result of the foregoing factors, economic progress of the country has been very difficult. Poverty, illiteracy, backwardness, and unemployment, are widespread. Problems of poverty and unemployment in the context of the people's, 'revolution of rising expectations' have given rise to public unrest and inter-group dissensions on the basis of religion, language, and region[3].

2 and 3 Requirements of Adjustment to Pressures of Change; and Problems of Identity, Insecurity and Politico-Economic Interests

The foregoing processes of change posed new challenges before the Muslims remaining in India. In the aftermath of the creation of Pakistan, large scale communal riots, and with massive movements of refugee population across the two countries[4], Muslims in India found themselves in a highly insecure position. They apprehended serious threats to their very survival in the new state. Soon however, they realized their political importance as voters in the democratic set up of the country. Their fears then gave way to their growing consciousness as an important socio-political group which could collectively exert political pressure for promoting its communal interests.

The problems of preserving their religio-cultural traditions in a changing milieu, however, faced the Indian Muslims. The community's response to secular education, and spread of modern ideas and ideologies through mass media of communication, has largely been one of insulation and rejection.[5] They mostly prefer to deny their children modern education. The problem of preserving traditional religio-cultural communal identity amidst powerful processes of politico-economic change, has generated a sense of collective anxiety on the part of Indian Muslims as a group.

4. Perceived Ethnic Basis of Self-Identity by Individuals

Muslims acquire their distinctive sense of communal identity during their process of socialization. Religious practices, symbols, customs, rituals, linguistic usage, dress, and early education in family and schools, instill in them perceptions of being 'different' from the members of other religio-cultural groups. Their 'life experiences' resulting from exposure to riot situations and ethnic media, and participation in communal social transactions and socio-political organizations, serve to strengthen their perceived ethnic basis of self-consciousness. Pan-Islamic influences from other Muslim countries also encourage their communal awareness.

Apart from religion (Islam), language (Urdu) has also emerged as a constitutent element of the Indian Muslim's perceived self-identity. Muslims in different parts of India where they have been using regional languages since generations, have declared Urdu as their mother-tongue, and demanded Urdu primary schools for the education of their children.

5. Attitudes, Beliefs and Perception of Interests Corresponding to Ethnic Group Identity

Muslims qua their sense of identity as Muslims come to develop an innate love for their religion, language (Urdu) culture, social institutions, and historical heritage. Their natural inclination toward judging national and local problems, issues and events from the view point of the community's interests, comes to the fore in their social interaction with others. Stronger the sense of their communal identity fostered through their socialisation process and life experiences, the greater the conditioning of their attitudes, beliefs and subjective images toward the primacy of their narrow communal interests.

6. Organization(s) for the Affirmation ot Ethnic Identity and Promotion of Group Interests

Muslims have a number of sectarian political organizations. Some of them are relatively better established than others in specific areas. More well known of the Muslim organizations are: Jamate Islami, Muslim League, Jamait-ul-ulemai Hind, Muslim Majlis, Ittehade-ul-Muslmin, Tabligi Jamat and Jamate Tulba.Accordinng to a report, there are now 553 Muslim organization in the country. They carry on political activities in an organized manner, publish newspaper and magazines, hold public meetings, and express the demands and grievances of Muslims in various ways. The national and secular parties also maintain their minority cells which ostensibly profess to look after the Muslim interests.

7. Sectarian Socio-Political Orientation of Group Members

As a result of their strong sense of communal identification, and participation in religio-cultural and political organizations devoted to the affirmation of Muslim identity and promotion of Muslim interests, large sections of Muslim masses come to acquire a sectarian mental outlook. In terms of such an outlook and thought—ways, they view, interpret, and adjudge every event, situation, and development in the country in a narrow and parchochial manner. The reactions and responses of the communal leadership in such context thence serve to manifest the phenomenon of Muslim communalism. Speeches and statements of Muslim leadership from public and communal platforms, and their writings in the ethnic media, render over their sectarian socio-political orientation.

Sectarian orientation of the Muslims acquires an intolerant and dogmatic religio-political character and on account of "a Muslim dogma of faith which preaches exclusive respect for Muslim as Muslim by Muslim (Ikram-i-Muslim)" (Durrany 1984). The Islamic ethos abrogates the message of past prophets and religions, and decrees that Islam is the seal and finality of all religions. It asserts that there will be no prophet and no new religion after Islam. Similarly, Baig (1973) also traces the deeper source of Muslim communalism in Islam itself, whose undue emphasis on conflict between Islam and non-Islam has led to an unfortunate deficiency of humanism in Islamic dogmas and precepts. Under the influence of such a religio-ideological dogma, "Indian Muslims behave as stateless citizens as if they are temporarily living in this country" (*Ibid.*, p.19). They tend to look to Muslim world for the fulfilment of their religio-emotional needs. The lure of economic opportunities and highly paid jobs in the oil rich countries of the Middle East has served to reinforce their Pan-Islamic sectarian orientation further. "All down the west coast, from Gujarat to Kerala, the Muslim population revived by earnings from the Persian Gulf Sheikhdoms, is only too conscious of the magnetic power of revivalist claptrap" (Thapar, 1982).

Perceived Grievances and Deprivation of Ethnic Group Members

Sectarian outlook of large sections of Muslim masses in the context of their serious economic difficulties i.e., poverty, backwardness, and unemployment, engender in them feelings of being deprived and discriminated on communal grounds. Impact of historical factors — both medieval and contemporary — on their subjective world-view, reinforces their sense of communal grievances: While other sections of the national populace react to economic difficulties in terms of agitations and demands for economic benefits as workers, farmers, Government employees, and teachers, etc.; the reactions of the Muslims develop and are articulated along the communal lines. Muslims subjectively perceive their situation as the citizens of a poor, large, and multi-ethnic country in terms of the deprivation of and discrimination against their particular community. Such a mode of perception and thinking also serves to engender feelings of religio-cultural and physical insecurity. The latter are reinforced by the recurrence of Hindu-Muslim communal riots in diverse parts of the country.

9. Political Expression of Sectarian Demands

Communal perception of, and approach to, the felt problems of their community by the Muslim leaders, leads them to demand the reservation of jobs for Muslims. The extent of reservation must be at least in proportion to their total population in the country. Other demands relate to special arrangement for the teaching of Urdu to Muslim pupils, increased use of Urdu in administration, and its promulgation as the second official language in number of states, government's 'non-interference' in the Muslim's traditional personal law based on **Shariat**, preservation of the 'minority character' of Aligarh Muslim University, special efforts to facilitate Muslim's recruitment to police and armed forces, greater political representation of Muslims in legislatures, and finally the demand for a 'Muslim Homeland' in India where the Muslims who are a 'separate nation' can live in peace and security.

Political expression of the foregoing sectarian demands by Muslim organizations is facilitated by the nation's democratic political system, and their realization of the importance of Muslims as voters. These demands are presented as the 'price' for Muslim's political and electoral support to the national and regional political parties in elections. The demands are variously articulated through speeches and statements in legislatures and public media, propaganda in the ethnic media and public meetings, demonstrations before and representations to State and Central Governments, and an assiduous fostering of contacts and links with pan-Islamic organizations in Muslim countries.

10. Reaction of Other Group(s)

The foregoing expressions of the communal demands of the Muslims, generate opprobrious reactions amongst large sections of Hindu masses. Although the latter do not form a coherent and organized communal group, their adverse reactions to the Muslim demands cut across caste lines owing to historical memories. The adverse reactions are also expressed in the form of speeches, writings, statements and editorials, etc., in the non-Government public news media in general, and the publications of organizations like RSS and BJP in the particular. Country's relationship with Pakistan also plays a role in influencing the Hindu reaction. Events like the mass conversions of poor Hindus into Muslims, and the activities of the secessionist elements in Kashmir, serve to deepen the Hindus' distrust of Muslims.[6] Hindus are not organized along the lines of a communal group perhaps due to their considerable regional, caste, and linguistic diversity, but the attempts in this direction have been underway largely as a hostile reaction against the Muslims' political postures.

11. Mutual Distrust and Tension

Mutual distrust and tension between the Hindus and Muslims run deep. They are rooted in the memories of history, the most recent historical event being the communal riots on a mass scale in 1946 and 1947, the creation of Pakistan, and the movement of millions of people across the two countries during the same period. Distrust and tension are the inevitable outcomes of the subjective world views i.e., the perception, images and beliefs of the two communal groups regarding each other. They lower the threshold of inter group violence. Communal politics, propaganda of hate, and perceived provocations, thence lead to the emergence of violence in inter group interaction. The subjective world views of the Hindus and Muslims about each other are outlined later.

Events like the large scale conversions of Harijans into Muslims by offering them money, and the lure of lucrative jobs in the Gulf countries serve to deepen the Hindu's distrust of Muslims and engender tension and riots.[7] Non - literate and traditional Muslims's non-acceptance of the family planning programme is also viewed in the same light i.e., as a part of the Muslims' 'conspiracy' to increase their population for their eventual take over of India.

12. Disturbed Law and Order Conditions

When deep rooted mutual distrust and tension between the two groups are rapidly aggravated by random and/or planned provocative activities, disturbed law and order conditions are precipitated. Disturbed conditions range from isolated incidents of violence, arson, and killings, to large scale and extensive riots, and destruction of private and public property. The duration of riotous conditions may also vary from a few days to few weeks and months depending upon success of efforts to check the escalation of emotionally surcharged situation(s).

13. Government's Armed Action

Armed action is initiated by the concerned State Government to end a prevailing disturbed law and order situation on a part of its territory. This action usually consists of deploying police force, and if need be para-military personnel in large numbers in the affected areas, arrests and detentions of persons involved in rioting and/or spreading disaffection amongst the two communities, imposition of long periods of curfews, and in extreme cases firing on the rioters and arsonists. Adequate and timely armed action by the government is essential to check the severity and spread of riots to neighbouring areas.

14. Costs of Conflict

Disturbed law and order conditions generate in their wake the costs of conflict. Costs of conflicts are incurred by the communities concerned, and the Government. For the Government, the costs are in the form of a loss of reputation, loss of political support from the aggrieved communities, expenditures involved in the deployment of armed personnel, and increase in the number of police personnel required for the control of disturbances, costs involved in rebuilding and replenishing burnt or damaged public property, and providing adequate compensation to the riot-affected persons and families.

For the communities, the costs are in the form of the loss of life and limbs of family members, friends and relatives, loss and damage due to looting and burning, adverse affect on the student's studies and careers, spread of diseases due to insanitary conditions in the riot affected areas, loss of life caused by severe difficulties encountered due to lack of medical care and the supply of milk and medicines, etc., during the period of disturbances, and starvation faced by the poor daily wage earners.

15. Government's Assessment of Political Implications

This variable refers to the Government's evaluation of a particular prevailing situation and/or the extant state of ethnic disharmony. Such an evaluation is affected by the nature and mode of the expression of their demands by the Muslims, the reactions of the Hindus as a group, and costs of conflict generated by the riots. The assessment takes into account the intelligence reports received from government agencies, views of the local leaders of the ruling party, experienced administrators, and the Government's own political interests and responsibilities for the maintenance of law and order. At a higher level, the assessment of implications also includes the impact of communal disturbance on the country's image abroad, and its relations with other Muslim countries. In the present context, the Government's dilemma among other considerations its possible loss of political support from one or the other community, as a result of its action(s) or failure to act in some expected manner.

16. Government's Policies

Government policies for dealing with communal disharmony in general, and Hindu-Muslim conflict in particular, reflect the Government's assessment of the extant situations, their relatively serious nature, and its own political interests and ideology. The impact of policies is however, often dependent upon the 'political will', and ideological commitment of the Government. Policies like the banning of sectarian political organizations, and introduction of a compulsory and uniform pattern of moral education, come under this category. They, in their turn, can materially affect the complexion of ethno-political activity over a long term period.

Government's present policy frame is governed by the secular and democratic character of the Indian nation. Hence, in order to be responsive to the demands of Muslims as a body of citizens, the government has been pursuing a policy of accommodation and conciliation toward the minorities in general, and the Muslims and the Sikhs in particular. As part of this policy frame, it has been placing Muslims in important official positions of high public visibility. It has also appointed a Minority Commission consisting of members from the minority communities like the Muslims and the Sikhs for examining any case of injustice, grievance, and discrimination against any minority community, and recommend remedial action to the government. It has also taken various steps for the promotion of Urdu language and literature. Its foreign policy is oriented toward demonstrably friendly relationship with Muslim countries and support for their causes. Seeking improved relations with Pakistan, and encouraging travel between the two countries are also oriented toward the same objective. It has also tried to reorient educaion in schools and colleges through a secularist interpretation of historical events and personalities, in the history and language text books prescribed for study. It also utilize the mass media under its control i.e., radio and television for promoting the themes of national integration.

Recurrence of communal riots and incidents in various parts of the country, and the Muslim's demand for a 'homeland', show that the policies of the Indian government have not been quite successful.

17. Government's Response(s)

This variable refers to the steps taken and the moves made by the government in response to the Political Expression of Sectarian Demands by the Muslims, and the Reaction of Other Group i.e., the Hindu public opinion. These steps and moves are the outcomes of the Government's Policies i.e., the secularist frame of its policies and policy decisions. Its responses have broadly consisted of the measures to implement its policies outlined under the preceding variable. Weaknesses and inadequacies of the policies, and their ineffective implementation, have resulted in the continuance of this chronic problem even after the creation of Pakistan, and more than four decades of national independence.

The foregoing empirical explication of the system variable for this problem provides the basis for its explanation and prognosis in terms of the system dynamics of fig.4.

EXPLANATION AND PROGNOSIS OF THE PROBLEM

Although the problem of Hindu-Muslim communal tension is complex, chronic, and important, its logico-rational explanation is clear. The variables, Perceived Ethnic Basis of Self-Identity by Individuals; Attitudes, Beliefs and Perception of Interests Corresponding to Ethnic Group Identity; Sectarian Socio-Political

Orientation of Group Members; and Perceived Grievances and Deprivation of Ethnic Group Members; and the processes underlying them, lie at the base of the problem of Muslim communalism.

The distinctive aspect of the problem here, however, is a continuously operative high value of the variable, Mutual Distrust and Tension in various parts of the country. The high value of this variable is seen to be prevalent over most of the locales of mixed Hindu-Muslim population all over the country.[8] The reason for the persisting high value of this variable would appear to lie in the respective world views of the two communities regarding one another. These communal world views have primarily been shaped by the medieval period of history of the subcontinent, and reinforced by the contemporary history leading to the creation of Pakistan, and subsequent Indo-Pak conflicts. High values of Mutual Distrust and Tensions engender Disturbed Law and Order Conditions at any locale where random/planned provocations injuring the sentiment, of either community occur.

Prognosis of this problem situation may be outlined as follows:

(1) If random/planned provocations against a community occur, and are perceived by that community as intolerable affronts to its 'honour' and 'dignity', communal tensions would be engendered. The latter would rise steeply leading to disturbed law and order conditions i.e., communal violence and riots if unchecked by any institutionalised conflict prevention/resolution mechanism.

(2) If in the event of a future war with Pakistan, some Muslims are detected as directly or indirectly helping that country, a serious situation of extensive tension and violence against Muslims may occur throughout the nation.

(3) If the activities of the secessionist Muslims in Kashmir, succeed, they would lead to a heightening of the Hindu-Muslim communal tensions and conflicts in the country.

(4) If Islamic organizations are seen to be engaged in a large scale conversion of poor Hindus into Muslims, their actions would generate serious communal disharmony, and may trigger off violent incidents.

(5) Muslim terrorism may emerge in India if in future Pakistan and/or transnational fundamentalist Islamic agencies

promote internal subversion in India through large scale in-flow of money and arms in the country. This contingency would be representable as an exogenous variable affecting the variable, political expression of sectarians demands by the Muslims.

(6) Given the continuation of the present state of affairs and trends, the communal riots are apt to continue to occur in the foreseeable future as before.

(7) With ongoing relentless population growth in general, and amongst Muslims in particular, the frustration and aggression of Muslims (i.e., Perceived Grievances and Deprivation; and Political Expression of Sectarian Demands) are not going to decrease. They would lead to an increased level of communal unrest if the economic conditions in the country worsen. Muslim political groupings are apt to increase the stridency and militancy of their sectarian demands under such conditions.

(8) In the event of a new persecution of the Hindu minority in Bangladesh leading to large influx of Hindu population in the country, the communal disturbances would be engendered in the neighbouring states. This contingency would be interpretable as the impact of powerful Random Provocation(s), producing Disturbed Law and Order Conditions, consequent to the high operative values of Mutual Distrust and Tension.

(9) If in the context of electoral compulsions and political interests, the wooing of Muslims and other religious groups as vote banks by the political parties continues and increases, the problem of communalism would become more intractable. It would lead to a strengthening of Hindu communalism.

(10) If, however, mutual distrust and tension between the two communities were to be greatly reduced through long term, sustained, and effective efforts, at local and national levels toward removing mutual suspicions and apprehension, then communal riots may gradually disappear. Such efforts would build up a stable pattern of the reciprocity of expectations, and institutionalized

mechanisms of conflict resolution. Such efforts and development are entirely possible. Their nature and significance have been outlined in the discussion on long term solution measures.

SUBJECTIVE WORLD VIEW OF THE MUSLIM COMMUNALISTS

The major characterizing over feature of the problem here is a randomly recurrent pattern of relatively short-lived communal disturbances over widely dispersed parts of the country.

These disturbances are the outcomes of the high level of Mutual Distrust and Tensions. The latter are the resultants of widely divergent perceptual world views, conditioned by the medieval and contemporary history of the subcontinent. The problem's analysis thence needs to focus on delineating the subjective images and beliefs of the divergent perspectives of the two communities.

Salient consitutents of the subjective world-view of the Muslim communalists in India may briefly be outlined as follows.[9] They embody the subjective images, beliefs, prejudices, fears, aspirations, and apprehensions of the Indian Muslims as a social group. They are oriented around the group's definition of its situation.

(1) Islam is the only true religion of the world. (Respect for, and tolerance of other religions, especially the idolatrous Hinduism is thence lacking).

(2) Hindus are basically Kafirs (unbelivers) who worship numerous false gods. The enlightened ones amongst them accepted Islam like our forefathers.

(3) Hindus are cowardly, treacherous, and contemptible creatures whom we have ruled for centuries.

(4) Muslims's religion, culture, language, law, food-habits, rituals, and customs are quite different from the Hindus. They are basically a separate nation.

(5) Muslims must not accept 'family planning' which is un-Islamic, and would also reduce their numbers and consequently their political importance in Indian politics.

(6) Muslims in India also belong to the glorious world fraternity of Islam consisting of some fifty nations of the globe.

These countries would pressurize and punish India and the Hindus, if Muslims are ill-treated in India. Indian Muslim's must therefore cultivate, develop, and extend their links with the Islamic world.

(7) Muslims must zealously preserve and develop their religious rituals, language, and symbols, in order to maintain and strengthen their separate identity in India. They must wait patiently for the triumph of Islam in India.

(8) Muslims face gross discrimination in the matter of jobs in public and private sectors. Their lives and property are not protected by the police who abet the Hindu communalists. Muslims' plea for reservation of jobs in the government services and police is ignored by the Government. Promises for the removal of their grievances are made at the time of elections only, and are forgotten soon thereafter. Muslims must hence organize themselves on a common political platform for the protection of their basic interests.

SUBJECTIVE WORLD VIEW OF THE HINDU COMMUNALISTS

Salient constituents of the Hindus' weltanschauung about Muslims as a group may in the present context be also outlined as follows:

(1) Muslims are potential traitors to the country and many of them spy for Pakistan. In the event of Pakistan's military success against India, they would openly collaborate with the aggressors.

(2) With the creation of Pakistan, all Muslims should have gone and be sent there. Pakistan expelled all Hindus from its territory. Hindus were also oppressed in the former East Pakistan, and are presently persecuted even in Bangladesh. This is evidenced by their periodic waves of migration from that country as a result of persecution and oppression.

(3) Muslims are bent upon increasing their numbers. They do not accept and practice family planning. The proportion of their population in the country has been steadily increasing. They want do dominate the country's political system.

(4) Muslims' demands or sectional previleges like reservation of jobs, proportional representation, and promotion of Urdu, are basicallly meant for weakening the unity and strength of the country. Together with their game of increasing their population, they want to create another Pakistan. Already Muslim political leaders are demanding a separate 'homeland' for Indian Muslims and reviving the two-nation theory.

(5) Muslims are highly intolerant of, and contemptuous toward, Hindus and their religion and culture. They are very aggressive and have not adjusted themselves to Hindu-majority democratic rule in the country after partition. This is brought out by their insolent attacks on Hindu religious processions. In most cases, riots are started by Muslim bigots and when Hindus retaliate, Muslim leaders and politicians with their eye on Muslim votes, blame the Hindus.

(6) As a part of the Muslims' long term conspiracy to islamize India and dominate the Hindus, Arab money is coming to India for converting the poor Hindus into Muslims.

(7) The Muslims are mlechchas (unclean and low human creatures). They are brutal fanatics by nature and lack finer feelings. They understand only the language of force.

(8) The treachery and bigotedness of the Muslims is also clear from what is happening in Kashmir. Despite the enormous sacrifice of men and money made by the country for the Muslims in Kashmir, the pro-Pakistani traitors and secessionists there have driven out the Hindus from the state, and want to merge the state with Pakistan.

THE CONFLICT OF PERCEPTIONS

The perceptual divergence between the respective world views of the Muslims and Hindus is thus seen to be very wide. It underlies the basic nature of the Hindu-Muslim communal conflict. It accounts for the persisting high value of Mutual Distrust and Tensions between the two groups, and thereby engenders the recurrence of communal riots.

Subjective perceptions are extremely resistant to psychological change. In this context, communication measures in a long term perspective have to influence the socialization, and life experiences of individuals. For this purpose, compulsory education should be given to children emphasizing (i) respect for all religions, (ii) the essential oneness and unity of mankind and (iii) the need for the universal values of human ethics in the context of social life.

Importance of religio-humanistic values, and divine orientation of man should be stressed in a sustained manner through education and mass media. People should also be led to realize their significance for mental and social health. Religio-spiritual value orientation protects a man from mental disturbances e.g., tensions, worry, neurosis, psychosis, manias, depression and suicide, etc., It also protects his social health by overcoming the pollution of intolerance and bigotry, conflict and violence, crime and oppression. People of the country should be educated to distinguish carefully the spiritual values and moral principles of a religion, from the social practices regarded as religious or pertaining to that religion. The former i.e., the values and principles are transcendental and eternal, whereas, the latter may be mere outcomes of historical conditions and circumstances.[10] In this manner, they may begin to appreciate and internalize the universality of man's spiritual and moral concerns.

References

1. Girilal Jain, 'Hidden hand behind the riots' *The Times of India*, New Delhi, August 17, 1980; K. Vikram Rao, 'Factors behind Moradabad', *Ibid.*, Aug. 20, 1980.
2. For an account of the fanatic blind outburst of anti-Hindu comunal riots way back in 1921 in Malabar see Chaudhuri (1975). Here some obscurantist Mullas and Maulvis taught the Moplah's (Muslims of Malabar) "To hate all Hindus as Kafirs whether the latter had any hand or not in oppressing them like the Jenmies" (landlords) (p. 16). The result was murder of Hindus on a large scale, destruction or desecration of their houses and temples, numerous cases of forcible conversion, and outrages on women.
3. Fifteen million people moved across the western border only. Millions later came to India from East-Pakistan.
4. See for example a news write-up in the *The Times of India*, New Delhi, dated December 27th, 1983 under the title, 'Muslims neglect modern education'. The following paras quoted from the write-up bring out the issues involved:
   "—(The), secretary of the minorities commission says that Muslims are 10 times more educationally backward than other communities in the country".

"Educational backwardness is the root cause of their economic backwardness" he says in a report on the "public employment and educational backwardness among Muslims in India".

Muslim scholars consider the influence of western culture and modern education as a "threat to Islam". This is the reason that many Islamic institutes, including Dar-Ul- Uloom, Deoband and Nadwat-ul-Ulema have excluded English from their syllabi.

Some orthodox Muslims even refuse to send their daughters to English-medium schools as they feel that "Muslims educated in English-medium schools lose their identity".——— (He) has held Muslim leadership responsible for the educational and economic backwardness of the community. "Muslim leaders are obsessed with non-issues like Aligarh Muslim University, Muslim personal law and Urdu". A survey conducted in 430 Muslim-managed schools shows that Muslim students had a high drop-out rate after the 10th class. Their number at the graduate level in these schools and colleges is far less than that of non-Muslims.

He further says that wherever Muslims share territory with other communities they had remained backward. Even in countries like Egypt, Nigeria, Malaysia, and Indonesia, Muslims have remained far behind in education, industry, and scientific profession than Chinese and Christians——.

The secretary wants Muslims to change their outlook. If they are not going to change, he says, they will continue to suffer from communal and social degeneration.

5. A sample of the Hindus reaction against and their distrust of the Muslims, is given in the following extracts from a rather long letter to the editor published in *The Times of India*, New Delhi, dated July 6, 1983, p. 6:

"—— Muslims in India still regard themselves as members of an international 'millat' whose interests must over side the interests of the country in which they live. They have no use for such a "tawdry" value as territorial patriotism. That— explains the behaviour of Indian Muslims over the Al-Aksa mosque incident.

Hindus of Hyderabad had no hand in what happened to that mosque in Jerusalem. But Muslims of Hyderabad staged a riot, stabbed their Hindu neighbours, and desecrated Hindu temples. No Arab country came forward to chide the Indian Muslims for this infantile behaviour. But the same Arabs became highly agitated when the native people of Assam started objecting to Muslim infiltrators from across the broder. This was a clear transgression of international norms.

The government of India is playing with fire by pandering to this pan-Islamic patriotism of the Indian Muslims on the one hand and to patronising Arab attitudes on the other. The chickens have already started coming home to roost in Kashmir where the Arabs, the Iranians and other Islamic countries are pouring in money as well as mullahs in order to convert that integral part of Bharat into an independent Islamic theocracy."

6. See for example the news items like, 'Gulf money backing conversions, *The Times of India*, New Delhi dated Jan. 6, 1948; 'Lure of Gulf jobs behind

conversions', *The Hindustan Times*, New Delhi, dated January 10, 1984, as well as, a host of other articles in the news magazines of this period.

7. The real cause of frequent outbreak of communal riots in Malegaon and elsewhere is, in my opinion, **complete breakdown of mutual trust between the two communities**, which in turn, has been the direct outcome of the complex combination of (religious, economic, historical and cultural) factors–(emphasis supplied) Letter to Editor published in *The Times of India*, New Delhi, July 19, 1983.

8. The elements outlined here are drawn from the writings and statements of the Muslim traditionalists and 'non-secular' leaders. They represent the oft-repeated explicit and implicit themes in the Muslim ethnic media.

9. Baig (1973) makes this point in his discussion about the source of Muslim communalism being within the Islamic precepts themselves. The latter emphasize unduly the confilict between Islam and non-Islam, and thence serve to negate and obscure the essential humanism and piety of Islam. According to him, the believing Muslim should be guided by the spiritual values and moral principles of Islam, but not bound by the orthodox practices that may have been appropriate to the times in which they evolved, but are not necessarily valid for Indian Muslims in Modern time.

   The religio-cultural rigidity, insularity, and exclusivism of Muslims as a national community, and their identification with a larger Pan-Islamic community, prevent their adjustment withint a plural society. They do not accord primacy to their role as citizens of their country, and tend to have an extra-territorial loyalty. Inter-group tensions are generated as a consequence. The responses of Muslims to such situations are their political demands for exclusivist communal benefits on the one hand, and/or a separate state, on the other. Such a pattern of inter-group behaviour of Muslims is observable in other South Asian countries also (Singh, 1992). In Burma, Rohongiyas want to establish an independent Islamic state in Arakan. In Phillipines, Moros in Mindanao-Sulu are fighting for separation from the country. In Thailand, Muslims in the four southern provinces are demanding an independent Islamic State. The resultant tensions, conflicts, frustrations, and suffering, tend to entrap the community in a warped web of hate, rage, aggression, and despair. They in turn thwart the socio-economic development of the community, and lock it in regressive behaviour. Only a focus on the superordinate values of sulh-e-kul (peace and goodwill)), may help the community to free itself from the psycho-social entrapment engendered by its insularity and communal chauvinism (Ahmad, 1982).

BIBLIOGRAPHY

Ahmad, A., *Religion and Politics in Muslim Society*, Cambridge University Press, Cambridge, 1982 (Reprinted by Vikas Publishers, New Delhi 1983).

Abelson, R., and Bernstein A., 'A Computer Simulation Model of Community Referendum Controversies', *The Public Opinion Quarterly*, Vol. 27, Spring 1963

Ashby, W.R., *An Introduction to Cybernetics*, Chapman & Hall, London, 1956.

Baig, M., *The Muslim Dilemma in India*, Vikas Publishing House, New Delhi, 1973.

Balu, S., *Living Divinity*, Sawbridge Enterprises Ltd., London, 1981. (Indian edition published by S.B. Publications, Bangalore 1983).

Bill, J. and Leiden, C., *Politics in the Middle East*, Little Brown & Co., Boston, 1984 (2nd ed.).

Braun, M. *et al*, *Differential Equation Models*, Vol. I, Springer Verlag, 1983.

Chaudhary, S., *Moplah Uprising*, Agam Prakshan, Delhi, 1975.

Chib, S., 'Assam Problem: A Geo-Political Analysis' *Asian Profile, Vol. 10, No. 2, April, 1982.*

Curtis, M. (ed.), *Religion and Politics in the Middle East*, West View Press, Boulder, 1981.

Das, A., *Assam's Agony: A Socio-Economic and Political Analysis*, Lancet Publishers, New Delhi, 1982.

Das S., 'Immigration and demographic transformatin of Assam, 1891-1981', *Economic and Political Weekly*, Vol. 15, no. 19, May 10, 1980.

Devine, P. and Raflko, R., 'On Terror' in *The Annals of the American Academy of Political and Social Science*, Vol. 463, September 1982.

Deitchman, S., 'A Lanchester model for guerrilla war fare', *Operations Research*. Vol. 10, 1962.

Dixit, A., 'The Seraikistan move" *The Hindustan Times*, New Delhi, January 23, 1992.

Dixit, P., *Communalism—A Struggle for Power*, Orient Longman, New Delhi, 1975.

Durkheim, E. and Mauss, M., 'Dequelques formes primitives dę classification' L' Annee *Sociologique* 6,1901-2, pp. 1-72

Durrany, K., 'Dilemma of identity dogs Indian Muslims', *The Hindustan Times*, New Delhi, dated January 10, 1984, p.17.

D'Souza, V., 'An Analysis of Communal Tension in Punjab' *Economic and Political Weekly*, May 8, 1982.

Fanibunda, E., *Vision of the Divine*, Published by the author at Bombay, 1976.

Festinger, L., A Theory of Cognitive *Dissonance*, Row & Peterson Evanston, Ill., 1957?.

Fishbein, M. and Ajzen I., *Belief, Attitude, Intention and Behaviour: An Introduction to Theory and Research*, Addison - Wesley, Reading, Mass. 1975.

Fromkin, D., 'The Strategy of Terrorism', *Foreign Affairs*, Vol. 53, 1975.

Frankl, V., 'Nothing But: On Reductionism and Nihilism', *Encounter*, November, 1969.

Ganapati, R., *Baba: Satya Sai*, Part I, Satya Jyoti, Madras, 1981.

Gilmour, D., *Lebanon*, St. Martin's Press, New York, 1983.

Gokale, V., *Bhagwan Sri Sathya Sai Baba (An Interpretation)*, Abhinav Publications, New Delhi, 1975.

Gokale, V., *In Defence of Jesus Christ and Other Avatars*, M. Gulab Singh & Sons (P) Ltd., New Delhi, 1979.

Greelay, A., 'What is Ethnicity? in *the bulletin of the American Academy of Arts and Sciences*, Vol. XXVII, No. 8, May 1974.

Guha, A., 'Little Nationalism Turned Chauvinist: Assam's Anti-foreigner Upsurge', *The Economic and Political Weekly*, Special No., October 1980.

Gupta, S., *Assam: A Valley Divided*, Vikas Publishers, New Delhi, 1983.

Gurr, T., *et al.*, 'World patterns and correlates of conflict' in *Handbook of Political Conflict* (edited by Gurr), The Free Press, New York, 1980.

Hanfstaengl, E., *Unheard Witness*, J.B. Lippincott Co., New York, 1957.

Harman, S., *Plight of Muslims in India*, D.L. Publications, London, 1975.

Hazelip, A., *Twelve Tenets of Terrorism: An Assessment of Theory and Practice*; University Micro-films International, Ann Arbor, MI, 1980.

Heider, F., *The Psychology of Interpersonal Relations*, John Wiley, New York, 1958.

Hejmadi, D., *Voice of the Avatar*, Vols, I and II, Sri Sathya Sai Books and Publications, Prashanthi Nilayam (A.P), 1980.

Hibbs, D., *Mass Political Violence : A Cross-National Causal Analysis*, John Wiley, New York, 1973.

Hitler, H., *Mein Kampf*, Ralph Mannheim Translation, Houghton Miffin Co., Boston, 1943.

Ignatius, D., 'How to Rebuild Lebanon', *Foreign Affairs*, Summer 1983.

Inkeles, A., *What is Sociology?* Prentice Hall, Englewood Cliffs, N.J., 1954.

Jenkins, B., 'Statement about Terrorism', in *ANNALS*, AAPSS, Vol. 463, September, 1982..

Jordan, W., *White Over Black*, Pelican Books, London, 1969.

Kasturi, N. (ed.), *Sathya Sai Speaks*, Vols., I to XI, Sri Sathya Sai Education & Publication Foundation, Prashanthi Nilayam (A.P.) 1958-1988.

" *Sathyam, Shivam, Sundaram: The Life of Bhagwan Sri Sathya Sai Baba*, Vols, I to IV, Sri Sathya Sai Books & Publications, Prashanthi Nilayam (A.P.), 1960-1980.

" *The Loving God*, Sri Sathya Sai Books & Publication, Prashanthi Nilayam (A.P.), 1982.

Khan, R., 'Understanding India's Communal Politics' *Mainstream*, March 1, 1969.

Lecky.P., *Self-Consistency: A Theory of Personality*. The Shoe String Press, Inc. New York, 1961.

Lowenberg, R., *The Heart of Sai*, Whitefield, Bangalore, 1981.

" , *At the Feet of Sai, India Book House Bombay, 1983 (Reprint).*

Mannheim, K., *Ideology and Utopia*, Harcourt Brace, New York. 1936.

Maslow, A., *Motivation and Personality*, Harper & Row, New York, 1954.

McQuail, D., *Mass Communicaion Theory*, Sage Publication, California, 1983.

Mohsin, S., *Attitude-Concept*, Formation and Change, 'Wiley Eastern, New Delhi, 1990.

Moore Jr., B., *Reflections on the Causes of Human Misery and Upon Certain Proposals to Eliminate Them*, Allen Lane, The Penguin Press, London, 1972.

Murphet, H., *Sai Baba: Man of Miracles*, Macmillan, Madras, 1972.

" , *Sai Baba Avtar*, Macmillan, Madras, 1978.

, *The Glory of Avtar*, Macmillan, Madras 1982.

Murthy, M., *The Greatest Adventure - From Sai to Sai*, Sri Sathya Sai Books & Publications, Prashanthi Nilayam, (A.P.), 1983.

Murthy, T., *Assam, The Difficult Years*, Himalyan Books, New Delhi, 1983.

Nagarkar, V., *Genesis of Pakistan*, Allied Publishers, New Delhi 1974.

Nehru, J., *The Discovery of India*, Signet Press, Calcutta, 1945.

Patterson, O., 'What is Ethnicity? in *The Bulletin of the American Academy of Arts and Sciences* Vol. XXVII, No. 8, May, 1974.

Rajkhowa, N., 'Assam: Turn in the Tide' *Mainstream*, February, 1984.

Rastogi, P.N., *The Nature and Dynamics of Factional Conflict*, Macmillan, New Delhi, 1975.

" , *The Behaviour of Societal Systems*, Indian Institute of Advanced Study, Simla, 1978.

" , *Social and Management Cybernetics*, Affiliated East-West Press New Delhi, 1979.

" , *Intelligent Management Systems*, Affiliated East-West Press New Delhi, 1987

" , 'Explanation, Prediction and Problem Solving in Social Systems - The Problem of Ethnic Tensions in National Societies' (PART 1), *Kybernetes*, Vol. No. 12, 3. 1983.

" , 'Explanation, Prediction & Problem Solving in Social Systems - The Problem of Ethnic Tension in National Societies', (PART 2), *Kybernates*,. Vol.12, No. 4, 1983.

" , 'Human Misery in Social Systems: The Problematique and a Solution Approach', Guru Nanak Journal of Sociology, Vol. 4, No. 2, 1983(a).

" 'Reconstruction of Social Systems' *Guru Nanak Journal of Sociology*, Vol. 5, No.1 and 2, 1984.

" *Ethnic Tensions in Indian Society*, Mittal Publications, Delhi, 1986. .

" , *A Prototype Expert System for the Problem of Terrorism in Punjab*, I.I.T., Kanpur Research Report, 1988(a).

" , *Productivity, Innovation, Management, and Development*, Sage Publications, New Delhi, 1988(b).

" , *Reshaping the Scenarios of India's Future*, Authors' Group, New Delhi, 1992.

" , *Policy Analysis and Problem Solving for Complex Social System*, Sage Publications, New Delhi, 1992.

Reardon, K., *Persuasion: Theory and Context*, Sage Publications, California, 1981.

Rosenberg, M. *et al* *Attitude Organization and Change*, Yale University Press, New Haven, 1960.

Rothschild, J., *Ethnopolitics: A Conceptual Framework*, Columbia University Press, New York, 1981.

Rubenstein, R., *The Age of Triage: Fear and Hope in an Overcrowded World*, Beacon Press, Boston, 1983.

Ruhela, S. and Robinson, D. (eds.), *Sai Baba and His Message - A Challenge to Behavioural Sciences*, Vikas Publishing House, New Delhi, 1976.

Rustamji, K., 'New wave of violence', *Seminar* issue on INDIA 1982, No. 281, January, 1983.

Rustomji, N., *Imperilled Frontiers: India's North-Eastern Borderlands*, Oxford University Press, 1980.

Sahay, S., 'Bihar - Violence a way of life', The *Hindustan Times*, New Delhi, January 10, 1992.

Sai, S., *Dharma Vahini* (Discourses on Righteous Conduct), Sri Sathya Sai Books & Publications Trust, 1982 (Sixth Edition).

" *Dhyana Vahini* (Discourses on Meditation), *Ibid.*, 1982 (Sixth Edition).

" , *Jnana Vahini* (Discourses on Knowledge *Ibid.*, 1982 (Sixth Edition).

" , *Geetha Vahini* (Discourses on *Geetha*), *Ibid.*, 1972.

" , *Prem Vahini* (Discourses on Love), *Ibid.*, 1982 (Sixth Edition).

" , *Prasanthi Vahini* (Discourses on Inner Peace), *Ibid.*, 1982 (Fifth Edition).

" , *Sadhna - The Inward Path,Ibid*, 1976.

Sandeha Nivarini (Discourses on the Removal of Doubts), Sri Sathya Seva Samiti, New Delhi, 1975 (Sixth Edition).

" , *Summer Showers in Brindawan, 1972, 1973*, (Discourse during Summer on Spirituality and Indian Culture for College Students at Brindavan, Bangalore), Sri Sathya Sai Education & Publication Foundation, Bombay, 1973, 1974.

Sabherwal, O., 'Punjab Crisis Point', *Mainstream*, March 3, 1984.

Sandweiss, S., *Sai Baba, The Holy Man and The Psychiatrist*, Birth Day Publishing Co., San Diego, 1975.

Saran, A., 'Emotional Integration of India' in *Seminar on Social Integration in India*, Institute of Social Sciences, Agra University, Agra, 1961.

Sarin, L.K., *India's North East in Flames*, Vikas Publishing House, 1980.

Schmid, A. and DeGraaf, J., *Violence as Communication*, Sage Publications, California, 1982.

Shah, I., *The Divinity Within*, India Book House, Bombay, 1978.

Salomon, G., *Communication and Education*, Sage Publications, California, 1981.

Singh, D., 'Bangla-Burma dispute over Muslim settlers', *The Hindustan Times*, New Delhi, Februrary 12, 1992.

Singh, K., *The Sikhs*, Allen & Unwin, London, 1953.

" *A History of the Sikhs, Vol. 2 (1839-1964)* Princeton University Press, Princeton, 1966.

Singh, P., 'Growing Separatist Trend' *Economic and Political Weekly*, February 4, 1984.

Singh, S., *Khalistan: An Academic Analysis*; Amar Prakashan, New Delhi, 1982.

Singh, T., *Satya Sai Baba*, Hind Pocket Books, New Delhi, 1976.

Siriweera, W., 'Recent Developments in Sinhala - Tamil Relations', *Asian Survey*, Vol. XX, No. 9, Sept., 1980

Swann Jr., W. and Hill, C.,' 'When Our Identities Are Mistaken: Reaffirming Self-Conceptions Through Social interaction', *Journal of Personality and Social Psychology*, Vol. 43, No. 1, 1982

Thapar, R., 'Revivalism with a vengeance', *Economic & Political Weekly*, May 8, 1982, p. 757.

Trotsky, L., *Terrorism and Communism*, University of Michigan Press, 1961.

Turk, A., 'Social Dynamics of Terrorism', in *The ANNALS, AAPSS*, Vol. 463, September 1982.

Upreti, P., *Religion and Politics in Punjab in the 1920s*, Sterling Publishers, Delhi, 1982

Vickers, G., *Value Systems and Social Process*, Basic Books New York, 1968.

" , *Making Institutions Work*, Associated Business Programmes, London, 1973.

Welch, S. and Booth, A., 'Crowding as a factor in Political Aggression: Theoretical Aspects and An Analysis of some Cross-national data', *Social Science Information*, Vol. 13, 1974.

Wiener, M., *Sons of the Soil: Migration and Ethnic Conflict in India*, Princeton University Press, Princeton, 1978.

Wiener, N., *Non-linear Problems in Random Theory*, (Lecture 8) Cambridge, M.I.T., Press, 1958.

" 'The Mathematics of Self-Organizing Systems' in Recent *Developoments in Information and Decision Processess*(edited)by R. Machol and P. Gray, New York, Macmillan, 1962,

Wriggins, W., 'Sri Lanka in 1981: Year of Austerity, Development Councils, and Communal Disorders'. *Aisan Survey*, Vol. XXII, No. 2, Feb., 1982.

Index